Principles of Data Interpretation

19. A norm-referenced standardized achievement t
material that all children have had an opportunity to learn.

20. Standardized norm-referenced tests will ignore and obscure anything that is unique about a school.

21. Scores from standardized tests are meaningful only to the extent that we know that all children have had a chance to learn the material which the test tests.

22. Any attempt to set a passing score or a cut score on a test will be arbitrary. Ensure that it is arbitrary in the sense of arbitration, not in the sense of being capricious.

23. If a situation really is as alleged, ask, "So what?"

24. Achievement and ability tests differ mostly in what we know about how students learned the tested skills.

25. Rising test scores do not necessarily mean rising achievement.

26. The law of WYTIWYG applies: What you test is what you get.

27. Any tests offered by a publisher should present adequate evidence of both reliability and validity.

28. Make certain that descriptions of data do not include improper statements about the type of scale being used, for example, "The gain in math is twice as large as the gain in reading."

29. Do not use a test for a purpose other than the one it was designed for without taking care to ensure it is appropriate for the other purpose.

30. Do not make important decisions about individuals or groups on the basis of a single test.

31. In analyzing test results, make certain that no students were improperly excluded from the testing.

32. In evaluating a testing program, look for negative or positive outcomes that are not part of the program. For example, are subjects not tested being neglected? Are scores on other tests showing gains or losses?

San Diego Christian College
2100 Greenfield Drive
El Cajon, CA 92019

19,80

Reading Educational Research

How to Avoid Getting Statistically Snookered

Gerald W. Bracey

Foreword by Jay Mathews

HEINEMANN
Portsmouth, NH

Heinemann
A division of Reed Elsevier Inc.
361 Hanover Street
Portsmouth, NH 03801–3912
www.heinemann.com

Offices and agents throughout the world

The author and publisher wish to thank those who have generously given permission to reprint borrowed material:

Figures 3 and 4 from *Guide to Research and Development—Iowa Tests of Basic Skills, Forms A and B* by H. D. Hoover, S. B. Dunbar, and D. A. Frisbie. Copyright © 2003. Reprinted by permission of Iowa Testing Programs, University of Iowa.

Figure 6 from *Put to the Test: An Educator's and Consumer's Guide to Standardized Testing, Revised Edition* by Gerald W. Bracey. Copyright © 2002. Published by Phi Delta Kappa International, Bloomington, IN. Reprinted by permission of the Publisher.

Library of Congress Cataloging-in-Publication Data
Bracey, Gerald W. (Gerald Watkins)
   Reading educational research : how to avoid getting statistically snookered / Gerald W. Bracey.
      p.   cm.
   Includes bibliographical references and index.
   ISBN 0-325-00858-2 (alk. paper)
   1. Education—Research—United States. 2. Educational statistics—United States. I. Title.

LB1028.25.U6B73 2006
370.7'2—dc22   2005034445

Editor: Lois Bridges
Production: Vicki Kasabian
Cover design: Linda Knowles
Cover photograph: © Jonnie Miles/Photodisc Green/Getty Images
Typesetter: Technologies 'N Typography
Manufacturing: Louise Richardson

Printed in the United States of America on acid-free paper
10 09 08 07 06 VP 1 2 3 4 5

Contents

Foreword

When we last heard from Gerald W. Bracey, America's most acerbic educational psychologist, he was losing a part-time job at George Mason University because, it seemed to me, the school couldn't take the heat that often follows Bracey in his scholarly travels.

I suggested in that column that the annoyance of getting fired would not slow Jerry Bracey down, and I was right. I have just read an advance copy of his latest book, *Reading Educational Research: How to Avoid Getting Statistically Snookered.* It is suitable revenge against his many tormentors, and for people like me still trying to figure out how to make schools better, a must read.

As a popular writer and speaker, with regular columns in two monthly education magazines, the *Phi Delta Kappan* and *Principal Leadership,* and acidic annual reports on the condition of public education, Bracey has been exposing statistics abuse for years. But I have never seen him put together all that he knows as well as he has in this book. It has some of the best explanations of educational numbers manipulation I have ever read, particularly on issues like SAT scores, year-to-year school comparisons, and argument by graph that are most likely to deceive us innocents. The book has Bracey's deft prose and sure touch with clarifying examples. I also appreciate the fact he trimmed much of his sharp ideological edge, loved by many of his fans, but not by me. He acknowledges several times that no combatant in the bitter education policy wars has an unquestionable grasp on the truth.

(Potential bias alert: Bracey mentions me twice in the book, and unlike his usual treatment of journalists, he does *not* gut me like a freshly landed trout. On one page he says no larger lessons can be drawn from a story I wrote about a D.C. family using educational vouchers, and on another he says my view of Advanced Placement programs shows that the same AP statistic can have different meanings.)

Here is a good example of the Bracey passion for clarity. He is addressing the difficult concept of correlation, a key to many misunderstandings of educational statistics and to most bad education stories, including some written by me: "We can correlate any two variables. Whether or not the resulting correlation makes sense is another question. Before everyone started wearing jeans, the Dow Jones stock market index correlated with skirt length. Shorter skirts were associated with good economic times and a rising market. Longer skirts were correlated with recessions. To the best of my knowledge, no one suggested raising hemlines as a means to boost the stock market. Similarly, there is a correlation between arm length and shirtsleeve length. Given *only* a correlation coefficient, though, it makes as much sense to think that increasing sleeve length will make arms grow longer as it does to think that longer arms will mean longer sleeves. In this case other information could be adduced to assist in determining which way the causal relationship would operate."

Here he is guiding the reader along the twisted path, with charts and other visual aids, that leads to understanding the difference between standard and scaled test scores and how to create the IQ scale: "Now you may be perplexed because I've shown the standard scores running from -3 to $+3$ and they don't look anything like the SAT that goes from 200 to 800 or an IQ test that would run from 55 to 145. But it's easy to get from where we are, -3 to $+3$, to either of these other oft-used scales. Watch closely. I take each standard score, multiply by fifteen, and add one hundred."

Bracey is a prolific and aggressive critic of No Child Left Behind and the rising use of standardized tests to assess schools and students, but he is too careful an analyst to embrace the most popular alternatives to testing without also giving them the third degree. One favorite of the antitesting movement, portfolios (samples of student work), is seen by Bracey as just another idea with problems. So you have a nice big portfolio envelope, Bracey says. What do you put in it? "Typical work or the best work?" Bracey asks. "Who decides what is best? Teacher or student?" What do you do, he asks, when teachers disagree about the quality of the work?

My favorite part of the book is his look at the National Assessment of Educational Progress (NAEP, rhymes with *tape*), sometime referred to as the nation's report card. It is a standardized test given to samplings of children across the country to determine how well American students are doing in math, reading, and other subjects. Its importance has grown as the federal government has gotten into the school-rating business, and some experts have suggested using NAEP, or something like it, to test all U.S. students.

Bracey says that when NAEP was invented in the late 1960s "virtually every education organization in the country rose up in opposition." Some might say those groups were clairvoyant, because they feared a national test would lead to calls for a national curriculum, which is pretty much what has happened. (Some people, like me, are happy about that.)

The instigators of NAEP, U.S. Commissioner of Education Francis Keppel, and legendary educational researcher Ralph Tyler, wanted to keep the new test simple. They just wanted to describe what students knew, and didn't know. But in the late 1980s policymakers changed NAEP's mission to finding how much students knew of what they *ought* to know. Experts decided what would constitute proficiency in math, English, and the other topics, setting a level Bracey and many others think is too high for some grade levels. He quotes a National Academy of Science's report calling the NAEP achievement level setting procedures "fundamentally flawed."

This is one of the few places in the book where Bracey cannot resist making a political point. He suggests that making NAEP the definition of proficiency for the nation could be used to make public schools look bad so our education system could be privatized by right-wing zealots. That doesn't make sense to me, but Bracey is correct in saying that federal education officials of *both* parties have been consistently bleak about the state of U.S. schools, even in the face of some evidence to the contrary. This may have more to do with bureaucrats seeking money and power from Congress than it does with any master plot against public education, but it is a valid point, and Bracey has made it better and more often than anyone.

Don't look here for cures for our test-obsessed culture. Bracey makes a more modest case for making tests more reliable, more understandable, and less likely to be taken as the final word on how your child's school is doing.

His best suggestion is adding courses in what he calls "consumer-oriented probability and statistics" to our curriculums. The first high school principal who offers Bracey a chance to teach such a course will get my vote for administrator of the year, or at least a medal for valor. Bracey is hard to handle, but his course would be great. For those of us beyond school age, this new book also provides that welcome exposure to Professor Bracey and the many things we still need to know about measuring what is happening to our kids.

Jay Mathews

This originally appeared as an online column on the Washington Post's website, Dec. 20, 2005. © 2005, The Washington Post. Reprinted with permission.

Introduction

In seventeenth-century England and France, some people took to collecting numbers they thought reflected the health of the state—births, deaths, marriages, and so on. They came to be called *statists* and the numbers that they collected were first called *political arithmetic* and then *statistics*. State, statists, statistics, an easy progression. Shortly after the creation of statistics, Benjamin Disraeli, prime minister of England during part of Queen Victoria's reign, declared, "There are three kinds of lies: lies, damned lies, and statistics."* Statistics have had to defend their honor ever since.

The original name, political arithmetic, is telling. People collect statistics with a purpose. Sometimes the purpose is to advance the common good; sometimes it's to simply advance the people who collected them or their agenda. Addressing an aide, Winston Churchill said, "The first lesson you must learn is that when I ask you for statistics on infant mortality, I want statistics that prove that fewer infants died when I was Prime Minister than when anyone else was Prime Minister" (Wainer and Koretz 2003, 45).

Misleading statistics abound. Some do little harm. "Minutes from Olde Town," read a lot of real estate ads here in Alexandria, Virginia. Well, my previous homes in Bloomington, Indiana, Littleton, Colorado, and Palo Alto, California, are also minutes from Olde Town. Lotsa minutes, but minutes

---

1. In America, this statement is often attributed to Mark Twain. Twain certainly popularized it, but he gave Disraeli credit for coining it.

nevertheless. *Minutes* does not serve as the best unit to describe the distance of those other places, and it might be misleading in some of the real estate ads as well. Similarly, many ads ask us to purchase something for "just pennies a day." Well, any dollar amount *can* be rendered in terms of pennies a day. Lotsa pennies, but pennies nevertheless. Readers should be careful to determine if the unit used in any research they read—ethnic groups, socio-economic status groups, schools, districts, states, nations, whatever—serves as the best unit for understanding what is going on.

An ad in the June 24, 2005, *Mount Vernon Gazette* told me, "You won't believe that this stunning house is under a million dollars." Asking price? $999,999. Really. My wife wanted to call and ask if they'd take $999,997 (given the real estate market here, probably not). Darrell Huff would call this gimmick "Much Ado About Practically Nothing." That's the title of a chapter in his 1954 classic, *How to Lie with Statistics.* That the book is still in print a half century later might tell us something about the state of the nation's statistical sophistication.

Huff opens the chapter with an example of two children, one with a tested IQ of 98, the other with an IQ of 101. The average score on IQ tests is 100. We could conclude that one child has a mental capacity below average, the other above average. Huff has a word for a conclusion like this: "nonsense." Actually, two words: "sheer nonsense." If you retested the children, this small difference might disappear entirely or reverse direction, with the IQ 98 child scoring above 100. And even if the IQs stayed the same, three IQ points is, well, three IQ points and nothing significant in either the statistical or the practical sense of that word (the difference between practical and statistical significance is explained on pages 68–71).

Many statistics that appear on the national scene are intended to shock and convince and are not so harmless. The Centers for Disease Control and Prevention offer statistics to show that we currently have an "obesity epidemic" in this nation. *New York Times* columnist Paul Krugman wrote that *Health Affairs* reported the "extra costs associated with caring for the obese rose from 2 percent of all private insurance spending in 1987 to 11.6 percent in 2002" (2005b, A17). The documentary *Super Size Me* observed the bodily changes in director-star Morgan Spurlock as he ate three meals a day at McDonald's for a month. Those changes are themselves presented as statistics—weight, strength, liver function, blood pressure, and so on.

Some argue that the obesity epidemic is just a moneymaking scheme by the pharmaceutical industry. By convincing medical groups to lower numbers that define such conditions as obesity, high cholesterol, diabetes, and hypertension, they create many more "patients" for whom doctors prescribe the industry's expensive drugs. On July 4, 2005, the Center for Consumer Freedom (sponsored by Coca-Cola, Wendy's, and Tyson Foods, among others) published a "Declaration of Food Independence," which began "When in the course of human events it becomes necessary for freedom-loving people to dissolve the bands which bind them to the Food Cops . . ." (Center for Consumer Freedom 2005).

The center dismisses Spurlock, saying no average person would eat ninety meals in a row in one restaurant. (If I were Spurlock, I'd try the same regimen in a soup-and-salad restaurant.) The center also offers up Don Gorske as a counterexample, a man in the Guinness book of records for having eaten more than nineteen thousand Big Macs, but who weighs in at a muscular 180 pounds and carries a cholesterol level of 155. The center does not mention that Gorske (a) consumed all of those Big Macs over a period of thirty years, (b) does not eat either breakfast or lunch, and (c) has a physically demanding job (Spurlock interviews Gorske in the movie).

The dueling statistics could be pretty funny if the issue were not so serious. I have elaborated on the fat wars for a reason: In many situations an advocate for a policy or program serves up one statistic as the sole and sufficient evidence. In reality, the situation is almost always more complex and more subtle and, to use a word of the moment, nuanced.

For instance, on consecutive days, both David Broder (2005) and William Raspberry (2005) used their columns to call on the Bush administration to abandon vague promises about the war in Iraq and provide what Broder called "Metrics of Success"—statistics—that would go beyond a "fatuous formulation such as 'We'll stay until the job is done'" (A25). Both listed many specific economic, security, and military indicators—none of which would alone be sufficient as the sole measure—that should be part of any list of metrics of success (neither columnist, thus far, has been as forthcoming in declaring that would-be reformers should also use metrics of success other than test scores to evaluate schools, teachers, and kids).

America's principal statistics problem is, as Joel Best put it in *Damned Lies and Statistics* (2001), "Most of the time, most people simply *accept statistics without question*" (4; emphasis in the original). One of the reasons we do so is that we are often in no position to do otherwise. We lack the information to challenge the figures. This creates an especially dangerous situation when we're dealing with what Best calls "mutant statistics"—statistics that began life as legitimate numbers but suffered mutation by someone or some group. Best observes that in the 1980s a report indicated that some 150,000 women in this country suffered from anorexia. Another study reported that anorexia can lead to death. The mutant—and widely circulated—statistic: 150,000 American women a year die of anorexia.

How many women die of what causes each year is not something most of us keep readily available in memory. Still, says Best, people writing the reports and accepting the statistic should have known better. A simple check of the *Statistical Abstract of the United States,* an enormous annual compendium of statistics from the Census Bureau, would have shown that each year about 8,500 women aged fifteen to twenty-four died of all causes, as did 47,000 women aged twenty-five to forty-four. But anorexia is typically a disorder in *young* women. Thus, if only 55,500 women aged fifteen to forty-five died each year of *all* causes, what were the chances that 150,000 women of all ages died of anorexia?

The good news today is that technology now permits many more of us to track down mutant or questionable statistics. Recently, someone mentioned offhand on an Internet listserv that in the original Cinderella story, the slipper was made of fur. In less than five minutes several members of the email list had definitively refuted that claim with information found using the Google search engine. There are, what, dozens, perhaps hundreds, of websites devoted to debunking phony data and urban legends.

Another problem, though, is that people accept many statistics because they lack the tools to think about them critically. Google and the Net cannot offer much if you don't know how to ask the needed question. The hope of this book is to help develop such tools in the realm of education, to help people become smarter consumers of research and statistics.

In spite of all the new technology, consuming statistics smartly might be harder now than it was when Huff was writing. Huff primarily concerned himself with statistics tossed around by Madison Avenue, then a synonym for the world of advertising. Advertising is a profession of deception, a world committed to making trivial product differences seem large and important and to convincing you that unless you buy a particular product you are incomplete as a human being.

Public schools in Huff's day were under attack, to be sure, and the reforms concerned curriculum, but there didn't seem to be enormous ideological wars over such divisions as whole language versus phonics or basic math versus rain forest math (although there was at least a spat about look-say beginning reading instruction versus phonics). Huff's book appeared the year after Arthur Bestor's influential *Educational Wastelands: The Retreat from Learning in Our Public Schools.*

Rudolph Flesch hadn't yet written *Why Johnny Can't Read,* nor had Milton Friedman penned *Capitalism and Freedom,* which contained the first contemporary call for school vouchers. Today, alas, there are many "studies" out there that qualify only as pseudoresearch, articles designed to provide something of a scholarly façade for an ideological message. Writing about this subject, Stephen Hegarty of the *St. Petersburg Times* said, "[Jay P.] Greene denies that he has become a 'Researcher to the Right.' Yet his work undeniably provides hard data and scholarly cover to policies driven largely by ideology" (2003, 1). I would dispute the "hard data" phrase—a lot of that researcher's data squish when pressed—but the rest of the comment is dead-on.

The May 18 issue of *Education Week* (Viadero 2005) carried a front-page piece on the debate over whether or not researchers should even release to the press studies that have not yet been peer reviewed (1). Such a practice is taboo in the medical field and should be in education, too. But it isn't. Peer review is not a foolproof process and it has sometimes been attacked as buddies approving buddies. My experience, though, is that it is more likely to be people in a field reviewing research in the same or a similar field. For peer-reviewed journals, authors are anonymous to the reviewers and the reviewers are anonymous to the authors; I have seldom been able to manage a guess about authorship of manuscripts sent to me by journal editors. Peer review assures a reader that experts in the field have found the methods sound and the conclusions reasonable.

Economist Paul Krugman traces the rise of phony research to Irving Kristol, a conservative thinker of the twentieth century:

> In 1978, Mr. Kristol urged corporations to make "philanthropic contributions to scholars and institutions who are likely to advocate preservation of a strong private sector." That was delicately worded, but the clear implication was that corporations that didn't like the results of academic research, however valid, should support people willing to say something more to their liking.
>
> Corporations followed his lead, pouring a steady stream of money into think tanks that created a sort of parallel universe, a world of "scholars" whose careers are based on toeing an ideological line, rather than on doing research that stands up to scrutiny by their peers.
>
> There are several reasons why fake research is so effective. One is that nonscientists sometimes find it hard to tell the difference

between research and advocacy—if it's got numbers and charts in it, doesn't that make it science? (2005a, A15)

Krugman considers efforts to discount global warming ("lavishly" funded by the energy industry, especially ExxonMobil) and to promote intelligent design as examples of this phony research. In education, readers should beware of "research" emanating from the Hoover Institution at Stanford University, the Heritage Foundation, the Manhattan Institute, the Heartland Institute, the Mackinac Center, the Center for Education Reform, the Thomas B. Fordham Foundation, the American Enterprise Institute, the Paul Peterson group at Harvard, and, soon, the Department of Education Reform at the University of Arkansas. Arkansas is home to the Walton family, and much Wal-Mart money has already made its way to the University of Arkansas, $300 million in 2002 alone. The new department, to be headed by Jay P. Greene, currently at the Manhattan Institute, will no doubt benefit from the Walton presence. The family's largesse was estimated to approach $1 billion per year (Hopkins 2004), and before his death in an airplane crash, John Walton was perhaps the nation's most energetic advocate of school vouchers.*

All of the above organizations produce literature whose "data" supposedly support the destruction of the public schools and the establishment of a free-market school system. The pros and cons of this debate are beyond the scope of this book, but the evidence to date does not support contentions that a free-market system would improve education. The National Center for the Study of Privatization in Education operates pretty true to its name. It is not a propaganda factory. Two of its fellows, though, surveyed the various privatization efforts of the 1990s and concluded that there was little evidence that they did work or might work in the future. "Disadvantaged students may not benefit from a free market of choice" (Belfield and d'Entremont 2005).

The media don't help much. By convention, they present, at best, "balanced" articles, not critical investigative pieces. In a 2004 Wisconsin speech, Robert F. Kennedy Jr. called the White House press corps "a pack of

2. It is interesting to contrast the Waltons' philanthropy with that of the Bill and Melinda Gates Foundation. Gates has backed the establishment of small public schools in New York City and recently put forth $40 million to establish seventy schools modeled after the innovative and hugely successful Met School in Providence, Rhode Island. The Met is a public school with no curriculum, no courses, and no tests that serves mostly poor students, almost all of whom graduate and go on to college.

stenographers." Krugman claims that if Bush said the earth was flat, head-lines would read "Opinions Differ on Shape of the Earth." More generally *Washington Post* ombudsman Richard Harwood revealed that 70 to 90 percent of journalists' content comes from what people in positions of authority tell them to write (1994, A29).

So you need some savvy about statistics and what they do and don't, can and can't tell you. For instance, one unreviewed study that was released to the press and public claimed, "Because these results are statistically significant we can be very confident that the charter schools in our study did have a positive effect on test scores" (Greene, Forster, and Winters 2003). My hope is that by the end of this book you'll be able to determine that this statement, no matter what the ideology of the people who made it, might very well be false.

You need some language savvy, too. One of these days I'm going to write a book on the language of propaganda.* For now, suffice to say that language that seeks to persuade, not merely inform, is suspect in a research report. The standards for such language are lower now than when I attended graduate school forty years ago. In my first report in my first year I presented some data and asserted that they represented "an interesting finding." The report came back from the overseeing professor with the word *interesting* struck through in red pencil and this note: "The *reader* will decide if it's interesting."

That might be overkill, but you get the point. Nowadays, researchers commonly call attention to results they find interesting. Given the blizzard of data from research, that eases the job of readers, but it can still mislead. Language that seeks to make up your mind for you or to send your mind thinking in a certain direction is not the language of research. Certainly terms such as *Food Cops, dietary despotism,* and *a growing cabal of menu med-dlers,* all of which appear in the "Declaration of Food Independence," do not impress one with their desire to reveal the unvarnished truth.

"Politics and the English Language," penned in 1946 by George Orwell, two years before he gave us the doublespeak and newspeak of *1984,* remains one of the finest essays on language savvy. Decrying "modern" usage, Orwell dismisses speakers of such as automatons:

---

3. On a whim, I entered "language of propaganda" into Google and got 504 items, some of them quite interesting. A lot of the first 50 or so entries referred to contemporary politics, the Holocaust, or *1984.*

When one watches some tired hack on the platform mechanically repeating the familiar phrases—*bestial, atrocities, iron heel, bloodstained, tyranny, free peoples of the world, stand shoulder to shoulder*—one often has a curious feeling that one is not watching a live human being but some kind of dummy. . . . A speaker who uses that kind of phraseology has gone some distance toward turning himself into a machine. The appropriate noises are coming out of his larynx, but his brain is not involved, as it would be if he were choosing the words for himself. (87)

Orwell developed a few rules for brain-involved speech that are worth repeating even in a book about research and statistics because the rhetoric surrounding statistics is often misleading.

1. Never use a metaphor, simile, or other figure of speech which you are used to seeing in print.

2. Never use a long word where a short one will do.

3. If it is possible to cut a word out, always cut it out.

4. Never use the passive where you can use the active.

5. Never use a foreign phrase, a scientific word, or a jargon word if you can think of an everyday English equivalent.

6. Break any of these rules sooner than say anything outright barbarous. (Orwell 1950)

In this book, the text, which must because of its subject use some scientific and technical words, sometimes leads up to a culminating point, which is then set off as a "principle of data interpretation." The entire list of such principles follows this introduction as a means of orienting the reader to the book and its contents.

This book is about data, and most of the data about schools these days comes to us in terms of test results, so the book contains an extensive section on testing. The testing section differs a bit from the rest of the book in that it provides some conceptual understanding about testing per se as well as some information about the statistics emanating from tests.

And at the end, the book provides a list of resources for exploring in depth anything mentioned on these pages. Hopefully, many of the works cited in the text will serve that function as well.

Principles of Data Interpretation

1. Do the arithmetic.

2. Show me the data!

3. Look for and beware of selectivity in the data.

4. When comparing groups, make sure the groups are comparable.

5. Be sure the rhetoric and the numbers match.

6. Beware of convenient claims that, whatever the calamity, public schools are to blame.

7. Beware of simple explanations for complex phenomena.

8. Make certain you know what statistic is being used when someone is talking about the "average."

9. Be aware of whether you are dealing with *rates* or *numbers*. Similarly, be aware of whether you are dealing with *rates* or *scores*.

10. When comparing either rates or scores over time, make sure the groups remain comparable as the years go by.

11. Be aware of whether you are dealing with *ranks* or *scores*.

12. Watch out for Simpson's paradox.

13. Do not confuse statistical significance and practical significance.

14. Make no causal inferences from correlation coefficients.

15. Any two variables can be correlated. The resultant correlation coefficient might or might not be meaningful.

16. Learn to "see through" graphs to determine what information they actually contain.

17. Make certain that any test aligned with a standard comprehensively tests the material called for by the standard.

18. On a norm-referenced test, nationally, 50 percent of students are below average, by definition.

19. A norm-referenced standardized achievement test must test only material that all children have had an opportunity to learn.

20. Standardized norm-referenced tests will ignore and obscure anything that is unique about a school.

21. Scores from standardized tests are meaningful only to the extent that we know that all children have had a chance to learn the material which the test tests.

22. Any attempt to set a passing score or a cut score on a test will be arbitrary. Ensure that it is arbitrary in the sense of arbitration, not in the sense of being capricious.

23. If a situation really is as alleged, ask, "So what?"

24. Achievement and ability tests differ mostly in what we know about how students learned the tested skills.

25. Rising test scores do not necessarily mean rising achievement.

26. The law of WYTIWYG applies: What you test is what you get.

27. Any tests offered by a publisher should present adequate evidence of both reliability and validity.

28. Make certain that descriptions of data do not include improper statements about the type of scale being used, for example, "The gain in math is twice as large as the gain in reading."

29. Do not use a test for a purpose other than the one it was designed for without taking care to ensure it is appropriate for the other purpose.

30. Do not make important decisions about individuals or groups on the basis of a single test.

31. In analyzing test results, make certain that no students were improperly excluded from the testing.

32. In evaluating a testing program, look for negative or positive outcomes that are not part of the program. For example, are subjects not tested being neglected? Are scores on other tests showing gains or losses?

1

Data, Their Uses, and Their Abuses

What Are Data?

Mull over the following statement and question for a moment:

> "When I think about data and graphs, I feel like . . ."

> "If you could answer any question about student achievement, what would it be?"

Consider the statement, adapted from Edie Holcomb's *Getting Excited About Data* (2004). Do you feel like throwing up? Anxious that a whole bunch of numbers you won't understand are about to come your way? Threatened? Does the statement put you in a problem-solving mode?

Depending on your past experiences with data, any of these are possible. Some people have powerful visceral reactions to the very idea of data. Others think of data as mysterious or as numbers that people can spin to prove anything (they can't, really, although speakers or writers often spin data in the service of some contention). When I served as director of research and evaluation for a school system, I noticed some people, notably some principals, tended to avoid me. I soon realized why: They were the district's insecure principals and I was the guy with the data. I could make them look bad. It didn't occur to them that data could make them look good, too. Other principals sat down with me often to talk about how to gather data that would shine some light on a problem they were interested in.

Now consider the question, adapted from Philip Streifer's *Tools and Techniques for Effective Data-Driven Decision Making* (2004). To answer this question absolutely requires the collection of data. Not that all data in schools are about achievement. We also have data about many other aspects of schools. But to answer Streifer's question requires data. Suppose the question is How can I raise the graduation rate in our high school(s)? This is a question that has taken on new significance lately for several reasons: (1) the dropout rate appears to be rising and the number of good job opportunities for dropouts is falling, (2) Microsoft founder Bill Gates has addressed and lamented the dropout rate in a 2005 speech to the nation's governors, and (3) the governors have undertaken to study the situation and to try to improve upon it, using some $15 million of Gates' money (although, I must say, if they continue to move in the direction in which they started—more testing, more accountability—they will increase, not decrease, the dropout rate).

In any case, to think about raising the graduation rate, we would need to know what the dropout rate currently is and what it has been over time (we'd have to agree first, of course, on a definition of *dropout*). Maybe it's already improving. If so, can we learn why and build on the improvement? All of these figures are data in one form or another. Why do people drop out? More data. What programs can ameliorate the conditions that lead people to drop out? More data.

Without question, the program both requiring and generating the most data currently is the 2001 Reauthorization of the 1965 Elementary and Secondary Education Act, better known as No Child Left Behind (NCLB). For student data, NCLB hangs its hat solely on test scores (with a nod to graduation rates). But to understand how NCLB operates, you need to know a fair amount about test scores. This understanding is addressed in Chapter 4.

Data Versus Capta

At one level of discourse, we should not speak of *data*. *Data* is the plural of *datum* and is Latin for "givens." But there are no givens. Statistics, the language of data, are human constructions and must be interpreted by other humans for the numbers to have meaning. This is often hard work. Suppose we get a report saying that the third grade in our school reads at an average grade equivalent of level 4.0 with a range of 2.2 to 8.6. What does this mean?

We will answer this in detail in Chapter 4 but we can see even now that we must know what a grade equivalent is. And why use grade equivalents? Is there a theory of reading growth that led some statistician or reading expert to *invent* the concept of grade equivalent? Grade equivalents can't be found lying under a rock in nature. Are there other measures of reading growth? Yes. Would these other measures paint a different picture? Maybe. Are these other measures harder to understand than grade equivalents? Yes and no, depending on what measure is chosen, but probably none of them is as *slippery* as a grade equivalent.

We might do better to use the word *capta* rather than *data*. Actually, *capta* is a word I made up. The proper Latin equivalent to *data* would be *captiva*—takens. Nothing is given. We take meaning from the numbers; we construct meaning. I use *capta* because it's shorter and pairs more euphoniously with the word *data*.

As mentioned earlier, some people say you can prove anything with statistics. It is more accurate to observe that different statistics sometimes lend themselves to different interpretations even if they claim to be measuring the same thing. We will see shortly that *mean* and *median* are both measures of "average," but they can produce wildly different averages from the same data.

Reading Data: Pop Quiz

Given that the nation is obsessed with statistics these days, it seems appropriate to begin with a pop quiz on how to read research. Answer the following questions.

1. In his column of June 23, 2005, *Washington Post* pundit George Will wrote, "Yet George W. Bush has increased the Department [of Education's] budget by 40 percent—more than the defense budget." Does this mean that the Department of Education got more money than the Department of Defense? (Will 2005, A27)

This twist by Will reflects one of the most common uses of statistics to confuse, namely to use a *rate* where a *number* would be more appropriate (or vice versa). If you have a big number to start with, a small rate increase will also generate a big number. The total appropriation for defense in fiscal year 2005 was $402,635,000,000. A big number. The total appropriation for the Department of Education in 2005 was $71,477,945,000. This is also a big number, but barely one-sixth of the defense budget (which includes some $20 billion for agencies other than the Department of Defense). Let's assume that President Bush increases the Department of Education's budget by another 40 percent before leaving office. That would add nearly $29 billion dollars to the education kitty. But if Bush increased federal defense spending a mere 8 percent, that would add $32 billion to defense coffers. A 40 percent increase for defense would add $160 billion.

Federal spending on defense dwarfs spending on education. Most education dollars—about 93 percent of them—come from state and local budgets. Counting all sources, we do spend more on K–12 education than on defense unless the cost of the war in Iraq is counted. The administration calls those costs "off budget." They currently come to $58 to 80 billion a year, depending on who's doing the estimating. If added to defense, that would bring education and defense almost to parity in total spending.

2. "The average SAT score for all students was 1014 in one year and it was 964 for those saying they were going to major in education. So the average student is 50 SAT points smarter than his teacher" (Martin Gross, author of *The Conspiracy of Ignorance: The Failure of American Public Schools,* in a speech on the book at the Cato Institute, Washington, D.C., on September 13, 1999). Any comments?

This is either one of the most masterful data spins I have ever seen or one of the dumbest things I have ever heard.[1] It uses the wrong statistics and requires some untenable assumptions, which are described a few paragraphs below.

What does Gross mean by "The average SAT score for *all* students?" "All" in this case is really about 43 percent of the senior class currently (a little less when Gross made his statement). About 43 percent of all high school

1. There *was* a wonderful moment in the talk, though, when David Boaz, a vice president at Cato who shared the podium with Gross, said that obviously Gross' findings called for expanded use of vouchers. Oh, no, said Gross, who then explained that his parents were Hungarian Jewish immigrants, and like so many sons of similar immigrants, he had thrived in the public schools of New York City and later at City College of New York. The public schools *made* this country, he said. The solution was to *fix* the public schools, not replace them.

seniors take the SAT. It is, at most, the average student in this group that is 50 SAT points "smarter" than his teacher (and, as we will see in a moment, this isn't true, either).

So the remaining 57 percent of the senior class are also sitting in classes with their teachers. How smart are they? We don't know. Some of this 57 percent will take the ACT college admissions tests, not the SAT. Some students take both. We can be pretty sure, though, that if we gave the SAT to 100 percent of the senior class, the average score would fall substantially below the 1014 figure Gross cites.

And those untenable assumptions? They are two: (1) All high school seniors who say they will major in education must major in education and become teachers, and (2) No high school seniors who say they will major in something else become teachers. We know assumption 2 is false. Many teachers arrive in schools with subject area majors along with the necessary credits from education colleges. We also know that students often change majors once in college, rendering assumption 1 false as well.

The U.S. Department of Education (1996) examined the smarts of recent college graduates, some of whom became teachers and some of whom did not. The general conclusion: "On several of the characteristics examined—including gender, college entrance examination scores, cumulative GPAs, or major GPAs, and credits earned in advanced mathematics, secondary school teachers did not differ from their classmates who had not entered the teacher pipeline. Thus the differences between teachers and those outside the pipeline represented differences between elementary school teachers and those outside the pipeline."

The Educational Testing Service found that prospective teachers who obtained subject-matter licenses through the ETS Praxis test series had SAT scores at least as high as other college graduates (Gitomer, Latham, and Ziomek 1999). Elementary teachers, though, scored lower.

So, elementary school teachers, but not secondary school teachers, do score lower on the SAT and ACT than students who do not become teachers. A question, unanswered and maybe unanswerable, is: Does this matter? Given the very different circumstances of elementary and secondary teaching, other personal qualities of elementary school teachers might be more important than their skills in the two academic areas tapped by the SAT.

3. "On virtually every measure, schools are performing more poorly today than forty years ago." (Martin Gross, same speech). Any comments?

"Virtually every measure" is not exactly a model of specificity. What measures does he mean? The National Assessment of Educational Progress (NAEP)? No. Forty years before Gross' speech was 1959 and NAEP hadn't even been proposed yet and wouldn't exist for another eleven years. The SAT? No. The SAT existed, but fewer than 30 percent of high school seniors took it, compared with 43 percent of today's seniors. The alleged superiority of the seniors in the past might well come from their having been a more select group. When comparing groups over time, you must take care to ensure that they really are comparable.

The Iowa Tests of Basic Skills (grades 3–8) or Iowa Tests of Educational Development (grades 9–12)? No. The ITBS and ITED existed in 1959, true. And, by Iowa law, each new form of the test must be equated to the earlier form (for many years, other similar tests were not equated from one form to the next). This permits comparisons across time. But if we make those comparisons, we find ITBS and ITED scores in 1959 lower than in 1999. So the one measure available to us contradicts Gross' claim.

4. "Among the 29 industrialized countries, the United States scored below 20 nations and above 5 in math. The U.S. performance was about the same as those of Poland, Hungary and Spain. . . . 'If we want to be competitive, we have some mountains to climb,' Deputy Secretary of Education Eugene Hickok said at a news conference Monday" (Associated Press wire story, December 7, 2004). Any comments?

Ranks often give one impression about performance while actual scores paint a different picture. Ranks force differences among those being ranked: In a race, someone must rank last. She can still be a fast runner as measured by her score—in this case, her time. In many of the international comparisons of test scores, nations ranked far apart have scores fairly close to each other.

Moreover, we don't really know what the differences mean. In the quote above, Hickok assumes, as many others have, that the United States cannot be competitive in the world economy unless it can raise its math scores. But the World Economic Forum ranks the United States as the most competitive nation in the world and it's not at all clear that there is a connection between a nation's economic health and its thirteen-year-olds' skills at bubbling in answer sheets.

Finally, I wonder what George Orwell would say about "mountains to climb." Actually we know: "Never use a metaphor, simile, or other figure of speech which you are used to seeing in print."

5. "When I compare our high schools to what I see when I am traveling, I am terrified for our workforce of tomorrow" (Bill Gates, in a speech to the nation's governors, February 2005). Any critical remarks?

Sometimes statistics are not needed to identify a silly comment. Let us suppose Gates lands in Lyon, France, and his hosts want to show him a high school. How often do you suppose the host would say, "Ah, monsieur Gates, we have zees really bad high school we wish you to zee. It is really 'oreeble.'" Right.

I once inquired about observer access to Japanese schools and was told by an American researcher who had lived in Japan off and on for a number of years, "Look, the high schools in Ozaka are ranked one to twenty-seven. You can get into one and two, maybe even twelve or thirteen. Not even Japanese researchers can get into twenty-six or twenty-seven." It is most unlikely that Gates' foreign hosts wish to show him even a typical high school, much less a bad one.

Uses of Data

Before discussing the various uses of data, we have to distinguish data from other observations.

Data Versus Personal Experience Versus Example

Some years ago I spoke to the Education Press Association. I presented many data from SAT score trends, NAEP score trends, achievement test score trends, and international comparisons to show that American public schools were performing at higher levels than they ever had in the past even though some schools in poor districts had horrifically low scores.

Albert Shanker, president of the American Federation of Teachers, followed me on the podium. In the program, Shanker's presentation had no relationship to mine, but given my conclusions, he felt obligated to say a few words about my talk before launching into his own. He recounted anecdotal reports of the shortcomings of American students, including kids who can't make change.

He ended with "Frankly, I find these personal experiences more powerful than"—at this point he waved his arm at the screen where my data had been shown—"all the numbers that Jerry put up there."

Had I had easy access to a microphone at the moment, I would have said, "Yes, personal experiences have two qualities. They are wholly compelling to the person who has them, and they are often wrong. They make a terrible base from which to generalize. That is why we invented something that doesn't depend solely on personal experiences. It is called *science*."

Personal experiences *are* compelling, and in many situations we *must* rely on them because we have nothing else. It would take too long to check out all of our impressions against "hard" data, and so we must often go with our gut feelings. But our experiences are, after all, *ours*, and we might have misinterpreted them, or, even if we didn't, we can't be sure that other people have shared them.

Similarly, many newspaper and magazine stories begin with an example. Examples personalize a story. In fact, *NEA Today* rejected an essay I sent to the magazine because I had written a general exposition of principles and did not begin with a personalized example.

The problem with examples, of course, is that we have no idea how well they represent the general reality. *Washington Post* education reporter Jay Mathews began a story about a mother in Washington, D.C., using vouchers to send her three children to a private school this way: "At 7:30 A.M. on a Wednesday in May, the four children of Nikia Hammond—Zackia, Asia, Ronald, and London—sat in the small living room of their public housing townhouse in Southeast Washington, straightening their school uniforms and watching TV while their mother put sausage and biscuits in a plastic bag for their breakfast" (2005a, A1).

The story describes how the children use publicly funded vouchers to attend a private school where tuition for the four of them would cost eighteen thousand dollars—more money than the family's annual income. Nikia Hammond says the private school has more enthusiastic teachers, smaller classes, and fewer discipline problems than the public school her children previously attended.

The story is probably true. Mathews is a careful reporter. But how representative is Nikia Hammond? How representative are her children? And, are her kids, and others using the vouchers, learning more than they did or would have in public schools? This story was written before the end of the first year of the Washington, D.C., publicly funded voucher program, so absolutely no data on that question was available.

Such are the limitations of stories based on personal experiences and examples. The better of such stories go on to discuss whether or not the example can be generalized but, as is the case here, such generalizations are not always possible. So, we move on to uses of data.

Exploring Group Differences

In PISA 2000 (Program for International Student Assessment) and PISA 2003, fifteen-year-old students in more than thirty countries took the same tests in reading, mathematics, and science (assuming for the moment that you can meaningfully speak of the "same" test when it has to be translated into many languages and taken in different cultural contexts).

We have gotten used to finding Asian nations at the top in these international comparisons. However, In PISA 2000, Finland finished very high, and in PISA 2003, Finland topped the world in reading and mathematics and tied Japan for first place in science. Finland's finish was all the more surprising to some because Finland does not use tests to evaluate students or teachers or schools.

Germany, however, which had long had the reputation (at least in German minds) of having the best educational system in Europe, finished low—lower than the United States, which was average among the countries. Most of Europe looked north to see what caused the Finnish success, and German educators flocked to Finland in droves.

Drawing causal inferences such as "*This* part of the Finnish system produced success" or even "*These* parts did it" is impossible. But one can look for programs and practices that could be reasonable candidates for leading to high test scores. For instance, although Finland begins formal schooling only at age seven, it has a well-developed, comprehensive system of early educational facilities. Teaching is a well-respected profession and teacher preparation programs admit only one in ten applicants. The Finns appear to have a genuine commitment to a no-child-left-behind approach, and schools that have difficulties get more resources, not punishment as they do here. However they teach reading in Finland, Finnish kids show a higher engagement in reading than other countries and they also check out more books from libraries (which are well supplied). The mathematics curriculum emphasizes real-life problems, and the approach to science is hands-on, two practices one could predict would lead students to do well on the kinds of math and science items found in the PISA tests (more about these types of items on pages 133–135).

The United States continually looks at group differences at home and tries to figure out what produces them, particularly in connection with ethnic differences and socioeconomic differences. A set of test scores won't tell you *why* groups differ, but it can point to group differences that might need exploring. NCLB, for example, forces schools to look at differences among groups. That might be its only good feature, in my opinion: schools cannot obscure the failure of some groups to achieve as high as others by pointing to high schoolwide averages and ignoring subgroups. (Again, of course, one has to assume that the tests used are valid measures of the topic being examined. Otherwise, the data might be bad and misleading.)

Fairfax County, Virginia, is a large (166,000 students) high-scoring district. In its magnet school for science and technology, the average total SAT score is more than 1500 (above the ninety-ninth percentile) for all students taking the test, and virtually everyone takes it. Some in the district, then, were shocked to find the test scores of African American students not only below all other groups but also lower than in some low-scoring districts. These districts where African American students are scoring better than African Americans in Fairfax might not be doing a better job of actually educating their students—at least some of them appear to have jettisoned any education that does not focus on what the state tests cover—but one knows for certain that Fairfax County officials will be exploring these group differences.

Sometimes, an exploration of group differences produces policy implications that are not apparent in looking at only the whole group. For instance, several years ago, the Education Trust set out to find what it came to call high-flying schools. It did this for each state using the state's test scores. It labeled as high flyers schools with 50 percent or higher poverty rates or 50 percent or higher minority enrollment (or both) that had finished in the top quarter of schools on the state's test in one grade, in one subject area, and in one year. Thus, if a school with 52 percent minority enrollment and 64 percent of its students on free or reduced-price meals had its third-grade score in the upper quarter in reading in 2003, the school was a high flyer for that year.

Note all the pieces of data in the above: percent minority, percent poverty, test scores, grade, subject matter, and time.

The Education Trust's study found high flyers in all states and made the case that if these high-poverty, high-minority schools could do it, all schools could. Thus they called their study "Dispelling the Myth," the myth being that poor kids can't learn (a myth I have never actually heard anyone espouse).

To me, the criteria seemed lenient—one grade, one subject, one year. The Education Trust put the data on its website as an interactive database that anyone can manipulate (go to www2.edtrust.org/edtrust, click on "Data Tools and Presentations," and then on "Dispelling the Myth Online").

I wanted to examine the impact of poverty, so I varied the poverty level only. The database will not permit you to simultaneously include more than one grade or more than one curriculum area. You cannot, for instance, search for schools whose fourth grade was high flying in both reading *and* math, only in reading *or* math. You can look at results for more than one year (the number of years available varies from state to state) and find, for instance, how many high-flying schools sustained that status for two or three years and, for some states, four or five.

From my perspective, the data, rather than dispelling the myth, provided strong evidence that poverty diminishes achievement. A lot. The following results are for California, but I have conducted this analysis for a number of states and they all looked nearly identical: as poverty increases, achievement decreases, dramatically (readers might want to conduct this analysis for their own state).

School Poverty Rate	# of Schools	# of High Flyers 2003–2004	2 Years	3 Years	4 Years	5 Years
All	4,914	1,260	949	823	740	664
>10%	4,393	677	485	398	342	291
>25%	3,716	249	139	109	79	58
>50%	2,693	38	14	10	6	4
>75%	1,479	6	1	1	0	0
>90%	639	1	0	0	0	0

The first column shows the varying poverty levels in schools. Column 2 shows how many schools there are in the state with that poverty level or greater. Column 3 indicates the number of high flyers for 2003–4, and columns 4–7 show how many schools kept that status for two, three, four, and five years.

We should perhaps be appalled first that 639 schools in California, the Golden State, have a student body where more than 90 percent of the students live in poverty. Only one of these 639 schools scored in the upper quarter of the state, and that one could not sustain its position more than one year. California has almost 2,700 schools with a poverty rate greater than 50 percent and only 1.4 percent of those (38 schools) are one-year high flyers.

What are the policy implications of these data? To me, these data imply that education reform would serve us better if we had a large, focused agenda to improve the performance of high-poverty students. Jack Kennedy did not say, "We're going to be number one in space." He said we would put a man on the moon within ten years, a highly focused agenda, and he put the needed resources behind the agenda to get it done. It got done in eight years. Theoretically, that is what No Child Left Behind is supposed to do, but it lacks the resources, the appropriate pedagogy, and, some of us feel, even the appropriate motivation.

Data and Theories

At the time this was written, some people and groups were devaluing evolution by calling it a theory, not a fact. This is true. Evolution is a theory. Science is all theory. Some theories are well supported by evidence (data); some are not. In science one does not prove a theory; one finds evidence that supports a theory by failing to refute the theory. If the theory is "All crows are black," every black crow you see is evidence for the theory. But, unless you know you've seen every crow that exists, it is still possible this all-crows-are-black theory is wrong. A single purple crow would disprove it.

Implied in saying, "Evolution is a theory," is the word *merely*. But all science is theory. Although much evidence supports them, Einstein's theories of special relativity and general relativity are still theories.

For the last seventy years, physicists have been trying to find a "theory of everything." Since the 1930s, they've endured conflicting theories of how the universe works. On the one hand, there is quantum mechanics. Quantum mechanics provides a workable theory for small events—things that happen at the subatomic level—but it is not so good at explaining big events—things that happen at the solar-system level. On the other hand, there is relativity. Relativity is very good at explaining big events, but not so good at explaining tiny events. There are also many questions that the extant theories have not been able to answer: What is the state of matter in a black hole? Is the speed of light the fastest in the universe?

Recently, string theory has emerged as a contender to be a theory of everything. At the present time, there is *zero* evidence for string theory, and physicists haven't even decided what kind of data would provide evidence. A scientific theory must be "falsifiable." That is, there must be some way, eventually, to gather empirical evidence to support the theory or not. No such way yet exists for string theory. String theory has made no predictions about the physical world that differ from predictions made from older theories. It is not even clear that string theory *can* be tested, at least here on earth. Tests might require matter to be in energy states not obtainable by even the most powerful particle accelerators. But no one puts *mere* in front of string theory. String theory excites physicists because of its potential. Theories can be respectable even before any data support them.[2]

Intelligent design is not a theory. It is a belief. Its followers believe that life is too complex to have evolved by chance. It is a respectable belief, but it should not be confused with a scientific theory. Evolution, incidentally, does not inherently conflict with religion generally. Nor, by many accounts, is it in conflict with Christianity. Science deals with what happens and how, not why.

Program Evaluation

When I was working in a school district as director of research and evaluation, a number of principals came to me and said something like, "We've had this reading program in place for about three years now and we'd like to evaluate it to know if it's doing any good." They seemed genuinely surprised when I said we should have started the evaluation four years ago.

The time to plan for gathering data in a program evaluation is before the program itself begins. Once the program has been around for a while without a planned-for evaluation, things get hopelessly confounded; steps that should have been taken to produce clear results often were not. Before the

2. If you'd like to read some truly mind-bending exposition on string theory, try http://en.wikipedia.org/wiki/String-theory. For a less theoretical treatment, try Dennis Overbye, "Lacking Hard Data, Theorists Try Democracy," *New York Times*, August 2, 2005, F1.

program begins, though, one has a chance to design an evaluation to properly show program outcomes.

Good program evaluation depends on design and on the proper selection of variables as outcomes. What, exactly, is this new program supposed to do? If it's a reading program to teach young children about plot and character in stories, you probably don't want to evaluate it with a test that concentrates on phonemic awareness and similar nontextual aspects of reading.

Tracking Growth

Currently, many people are interested in "growth models" or "value-added models" of educational outcomes. Although these models currently are afflicted with many technical problems, it is easy to understand why they generate interest.

The usual method of tracking growth is the consecutive cohort method. No Child Left Behind uses this approach. For a school to make adequate yearly progress, this year's third-grade students must score X points higher than last year's third-grade students. This is not true growth because the students are different (unless some students were retained in third grade, which further confounds the situation). A true growth model would track individual students as they moved through the system.

In the past, technological limitations have precluded the use of growth models, but the wide dispersion of more powerful computers and user-friendly software has allowed us to overcome some technological problems. Some states now have the capacity to find a given student at any time as long as that student remains in the state's public school system. More states are developing such tracking systems.

One particular growth model, the Tennessee Value-Added Assessment System (TVAAS), has received a great deal of attention because its developers have asserted that it can identify effective and ineffective teachers.

Two questionable claims have emanated from this model: (1) teachers are the most important variable in determining level of achievement, and (2) a student who has effective teachers three years in a row will show huge gains in achievement and a student who has ineffective teachers three years in a row will have his achievement horribly, irrecoverably, stunted.

These two assertions need to be carefully parsed to define certain terms and examine assumptions. Unfortunately, in many statements of the claims, no such parsing occurs—they are simply presented as true.

First, what is an "effective" teacher? The TVAAS defines effective teachers as those who increase test scores. In the original study, items from the Comprehensive Test of Basic Skills, an ordinary off-the-shelf norm-referenced achievement test, were used to generate the test scores. This surely is an inadequate means of defining *effective teacher.*

Second, the use of the term *level of achievement* in claim 1 assuredly renders that claim false. Family, income, community, and, yes, genes will play a more powerful role. The statement becomes more tenable if we change *level of achievement* to *changes in achievement.* One study found, as usual, that low-income students scored lower on tests than middle-income students—that's what "level of achievement" means. However, over a four-year period, the two groups' scores increased by the same amount. The changes in achievement were the same. Unfortunately, those who are promoting this claim of teacher potency use the word *level,* not *changes,* or they leave ambiguous which word is implied but missing.

Finally, because an effective teacher is *defined* as one who raises test scores, there is a certain amount of circularity in claiming that three years of effective teachers has an enormous impact on test scores. Even so, other research has indicated that tracing changes in test scores back to individual teachers requires unrealistic assumptions. It would be inappropriate to use the TVAAS to identify effective and ineffective teachers individually.

Stay tuned, though, because there is considerable interest in growth models. The Northwest Evaluation Association (NWEA) in Portland, Oregon, uses one in its computerized assessments in a number of western states and the U.S. Department of Education seems ready to fund some research on the possibility of using such models to measure adequate yearly progress in No Child Left Behind. The NWEA's model makes no attempt to link test-score gains to individual teachers.

Hypothesis Testing

People generate hypotheses all the time. Most of them we don't bother to test, but in the field of educational research, hypothesis testing is the principal activity. Some hypotheses:

1. Students who are absent more than fifteen days of school in grades 1–3 are more likely to drop out than students who miss fewer days.

2. Students who are exposed to hands-on science, including computer simulations, will have fewer misconceptions about scientific concepts than students whose science is text oriented.

3. Students taught to read with a literature-based approach will spend more of their free time reading than students taught with a decoding approach.

4. Boys who have names that are mostly given to girls will have more incidents of disruptive behavior in middle school but not in first grade. The number of disruptive incidents will vary with the number of girls in the school with the same name, and disruptive behavior affects the achievement of others in the classroom.

The first three hypotheses, while plausible, are propositions I just made up. The fourth is a "real" hypothesis that held up under testing. They all need some work in terms of making them more specific. For hypothesis 1, for example, we'd need a technology that would allow us to track individual students over almost their entire school career. We'd also want to check to see if the absentees differed on other variables. Did they do poorly in grades 1–3, which might indicate that school gave them trouble from the beginning, or did they do quite well, which might indicate that school bored them? We also should see if there is a good reason to set the cutoff at fifteen days—is there other research in the literature that suggests that this is the appropriate number?

For hypothesis 2, we'd need to narrow down "misconceptions about scientific concepts" to perhaps something like "misconceptions about the structure of an atom." For number 3, we'd need some reliable means of knowing how many hours a day or week students read when they're not in school. Self-report? Parental report? Both? A log?

For hypothesis 4, we also need more specificity and precision. What do we mean by "mostly given to girls"? The actual study defined it as more than 50 percent of the time. How would we know how many boys versus girls are named, say, Shelby or Shannon? In the study, the Florida Department of Health supplied the names over a period of years. What do we mean by "disruptive behavior"? The study defined it as at least one suspension of at least five days. Counting the number of girls in a school with the same name as a boy, the research did indeed find that the increase in disruptive behavior was least when there were no girls with the name and increased with the number of girls having the name. In a complicated statistical analysis, the study also found that disruptions lowered test scores of all students a few percentile ranks.

Everyday English is rich and flexible, but it often lacks the specificity needed to pin down a concept precisely enough to make it unambiguous in testing a hypothesis. There is a fine art to refining something like "misconceptions about scientific concepts" to an unambiguous statement. There is an equally fine art to determining what kind of instrument would be appropriate to measure our predicted outcome. Too often a standardized test is thoughtlessly applied.

Data-Driven Decision Making

Want to know the currency of a term? Stick it into Google and see what happens. For "data-driven decision making," I got 43,300 items. 3DM, as it's sometimes known, is hot.

It has also become in some quarters a term of opprobrium because it has been reduced to mean "Do whatever it takes to get the damn test scores up." Test scores certainly constitute data, and, as we will see in the section on testing, America is obsessed with test scores.

For me, and hopefully for you, data-driven decision making really means data-*assisted* decision making—using data to solve problems or understand what is going on. There is nothing magical about it or diabolical either. Edie Holcomb gives a humble but useful example. Teachers in one school thought that the cafeteria staff took too long to serve kids lunch, depriving the students of enough time to eat leisurely. In research we would say that the teachers had formed a hypothesis: the slow food service means kids don't get enough time to eat.

To gather data to test this hypothesis, the teachers looked at the menus at the beginning of a week for two weeks and predicted how long it would take to serve each meal. They consistently predicted it would take more time than in fact it did take. The hypothesis was false, but having the data let the teachers go away relieved and avoided a potential encounter with the cafeteria folk. The data in this case were actual serving times matched against the predicted serving times (Holcomb 2004, 83–85).

Another example: The High/Scope Educational Research Foundation in Ypsilanti, Michigan, has developed a Ready School Assessment (RSA). The RSA is used to study the flip side of school readiness. That is, American educators typically ask what they can do to get children ready for school, but the RSA looks at what the school faculty and administrators have done to get the school ready for the children. Schools have used the RSA to determine strengths and weaknesses in their ready-school activities and, in the case of the latter, to propose changes to ameliorate the weaknesses. Some schools have found, for example, that while they score high on the assessment indicators of the RSA, they might score low on Transitions or Parents as Teachers, both of which examine the extent to which the school reaches out to parents and the community.

Holcomb has developed a useful "motivation continuum" for why educators would want to use data to assist decision making (2004, 55). The continuum runs from purely intrinsic reasons to purely extrinsic reasons:

INTRINSIC

To satisfy our own drive for excellence

To reward and strengthen teachers' own feelings of success/efficacy

To be more focused and less fragmented

To demonstrate our belief that we can do a better job

To be more objective in decision-making

To test the assumptions we make about students and their performance

To give us a better idea of the "big picture"

To keep us from wasting time and money on things that don't work or don't matter

To present a more complete picture of the school to our community

To be proactive in reporting to constituents

To prove we're not afraid of feedback

To answer community questions about comparisons

To counter negative/inaccurate media coverage

To be competitive—e.g., non-public schools, charters

To respond to public press for accountability, e.g., federal, state, business sector

EXTRINSIC

Abuses of Data

The many abuses of data could fill whole books—and they have: *How to Lie with Statistics* (Huff 1954), *Damned Lies and Statistics* and *More Damned Lies and Statistics* (Best 2001 and Best 2004, respectively). What we can do here is illustrate the types of abuses. Hopefully, knowing these abuses will permit readers to more quickly identify them and less often get taken in by them.

Naïve Failure to Do the Arithmetic

This abuse occurs most often in examples that track or project changes in data over time. Historically, the most notorious such statistical assertion was "Every year since 1950, the number of American children gunned down has doubled." This example illustrates a common problem with statistical reporting: a lack of specificity. For example, how does the author define "children"? He doesn't say. It could make a difference whether he was thinking of ages up to sixteen or those up to nineteen. And what does he mean by "gunned down"? Where did the statistic come from? That is, who's doing the counting and why? Many social statistics have various methods for calculation, with varying outcomes. Agencies that collect social statistics often have agendas to advance that color how they define the variables of interest. An organization of environmentalists would no doubt define *polluting incident* differently than an industry-based organization.

The author of the "gunned down" statement is also guilty of misinterpretation. His is a distortion of "The number of American children killed each year by guns has doubled since 1950." The Children's Defense Fund made this claim in 1994, and it's quite different from the first statement. It says there were twice as many children killed by guns in 1994 than in 1950. It is still ambiguous: does "killed by guns" include accidents and suicides?

1950	1	1963	8,192
1951	2	1964	16,384
1952	4	1965	32,768
1953	8	1966	65,536
1954	16	1967	131,072
1955	32	1968	262,144
1956	64	1969	524,288
1957	128	1970	1,048,576
1958	256	1980	1,073,741,824
1959	512	1987	137,438,953,500
1960	1,024	1995	35,184,372,090,000
1961	2,048	2004	18,014,398,510,000,000,000
1962	4,096		

FIG. 1 Number of Children "Gunned Down" Over Time (Hypothetical Example)

I earlier quoted Joel Best, author of *Damned Lies and Statistics*, concluding that most people accept statistics uncritically. Many observers have commented on how Americans in particular ascribe to numbers an accuracy, precision, and objectivity that isn't there. It's an American thing. But ambiguity and distortion are not the most egregious errors in the "gunned down" claim. That prize goes to the failure to do the arithmetic. Let's assume only one child was "gunned down" in 1950 and that each year thereafter, as the claim contended, the number doubled. The results are shown in Figure 1.

These growing numbers are remindful of the ancient story of the man who did something heroic and was asked by the emperor to choose a reward. He asked only for a pound of rice the next day and twice the amount each day for a month. The emperor was dumbfounded by what seemed like such a modest request, but the hero was shrewd and by the end of the month, he controlled the nation's rice supply.

Given one child shot to death in 1950 and a doubling each year, the number of deaths would have passed the million mark in 1970 and a billion in 1980 (the current population of the United States is very close to 300 million). By 1987, more children would have been gunned down in America than the total human population in all of history (which is itself a statistic that is estimated, not precisely known; the Neanderthals were lousy statisticians). Remember, what the Children's Defense Fund really said was that between 1950 and 1994, the number of children "killed by guns" doubled.

Similarly, the National Reading Panel (NRP) repeatedly claimed to have received more than 100,000 studies in the course of its work. Given the duration of the NRP and a reasonable assumption about the length of the work day and week, this works out to about 1.6 studies per minute.

> **Principle of Data Interpretation:** *Do the arithmetic.*
> **Corollary:** *Check the arithmetic.*

People make arithmetical or typographical mistakes when copying numbers, so it pays to make certain that everything adds up. For example, in early 1993, as *A Nation at Risk* approached its tenth anniversary, *Education Week* analyzed what had transpired during a busy decade of educational reforms. Its conclusion: not much. Looking at various tests and the SAT trends during the decade, *Education Week* concluded

> The proportion of American Youngsters performing at high levels remains infinitesimally small. In the past 10 years, for instance, the number and proportion of those scoring at or above 650 on the verbal or mathematics section of the scholastic aptitude test has actually declined.

We could ask, Does it really make sense that a decade as full of reform as 1983–93 would have resulted in a drop of high-scoring students? (You should ask of *any* statistic, Does it seem credible in light of its context?) To corroborate its assertion, *Education Week* put the following numbers in the margin:

	Verbal	Mathematics
1982	29,921 (3)	70,352 (7)
1992	22,754 (2)	58,662 (6)

The small numbers in parentheses are the proportions represented by the larger numbers and it does indeed appear that both numbers and proportions of high-scoring students had declined (650 represents about the ninety-second percentile on the SAT).

But, because those numbers seemed suspect in light of all of the reform activity, I checked them against the "Profiles of College Bound Seniors" published by the College Board each August along with the latest SAT scores. The table that displays the SAT scores groups them in forty-point intervals from 200 to 800. So, one first sees at the bottom of the table how many students scored 200–240, then 250–290, 300–340, and so on up to a single fifty-point interval, 750–800.

The *Education Week* numbers for 1982 were accurate. Those for 1992 were accurate as far as they went, but they went only as far as the group scoring 650 to 690. The numbers for 1992 omitted all students scoring 700 or better, a clerical error, no doubt. When those who top 700 are added in, the numbers look a little different:

	Verbal	Mathematics
1982	29,921 (3)	70,352 (7)
1992	32,903 (3)	104,401 (10)

The numbers for both tests are up, and the proportion for mathematics has risen as well. In fact, the proportion scoring above 650 on the math had risen to a record high proportion. And it has risen to a new high virtually every year since 1992, topping 14 percent in 2004. Some have tried to dismiss the increase as due to high-scoring Asian students, but an analysis by ethnicity shows increases for blacks, whites, and Hispanics as well.

Check the arithmetic.

And, by the way, although I am certain someone at *Education Week* made an innocent, if sloppy, clerical error, the fact that that error made it all the way to publication reveals something related to a principle of data interpretation, something I call the Neurotic Need to Believe the Worst. If the numbers, any numbers, show public education in a bad light, they find much easier acceptance than numbers indicating something good or something improved. No doubt had the editors seen the real numbers for the SAT, those improved numbers would have been double- or triple-checked.

Deliberate Distortions

More insidious than statistics suffering from inept calculations are the statistics bandied about by people trying to convince other people to accept a point of view, a policy, or a program. For instance, in a *Washington Post* op-ed, former secretary of education William Bennett wrote, "Nationally, about half of all high school graduates have not mastered seventh grade arithmetic" (2000, A25).

This statement lacks specificity, too. We don't test high school graduates, so how could he know? We don't even test twelfth graders very often because they tend to make pretty designs on the answer sheets and in other ways blow off the test unless it's the SAT, ACT, or a test required for graduation. Bennett does not specify what he means by "mastered." Must a student get 100 percent of test items right to demonstrate mastery, or would some lesser score suffice, as it does for high school exit exams? Would the student have to flawlessly recite the multiplication tables through 12 × 12? Who knows what Bennett had in mind.

Finally, has the National Council of Teachers of Mathematics, the National Education Association, or any professional group reached consensus on exactly what we mean when we say "seventh-grade arithmetic"? I doubt that rather seriously.

The Bennett example leads to a general principle of data interpretation in educational statistics:

Principle of Data Interpretation: *Show me the data!*

This principle plays off a scene in the movie *Jerry Maguire*, where Cuba Gooding plays a football player about to enter the National Football League who hopes that his agent, played by Tom Cruise, can land him a lucrative contract. While Cruise is having an epiphany about the value of material wealth, Gooding keeps yelling at him, "Show me the money!" If you come across a statistical statement that could be considered suspect, you should consider it both your right and your duty to pick up the phone or get on the Net and ask to see the data that generated the statement.

In this instance, I called Bennett's office and was told by a staff person, "He got it from *The Book of Knowledge*." This *Book of Knowledge* is not a children's encyclopedia. It is the title given to a book of data—a treasure trove of slanted statistics—put together by one Michael Moe, at the time a financial analyst for Merrill Lynch. In the book, Moe encourages investors to put their money into stocks that make up what he calls "the education industry." Moe paints the performance of public education as miserable but claims that the private sector is gearing up to fix it. The seventh-grade arithmetic claim appears baldly without citation.

I called Moe. And I was told that its "an interpretation of some NAEP data" (2005). Trust me, dear reader, there is no way to get from NAEP to that conclusion without romanticizing the data beyond all semblance to reality.

Selective Use of Statistics

This is perhaps the most common abuse of statistics: choosing those data that, while accurate in themselves, reveal only part of the picture, the part supporting the author's agenda. The standard setter for selectivity in choosing data is the 1983 publication *A Nation at Risk*. Called then the paper Sputnik, and still heralded by school critics as a "landmark study," this sixty-four-page booklet is in fact a golden treasury of selected and spun statistics.

After its famous cold warrior opening rhetoric—"Our nation is at risk. . . . It is threatened by a rising tide of mediocrity. . . . If an unfriendly foreign power had imposed our education system we might well have considered it an act of war"—the commissioners who wrote the document provided a list of thirteen indicators of risk, twelve of which directly reported test scores and one that had an indirect bearing on test scores. A couple of examples:

"There was a steady decline in science achievement scores of U.S. 17-year-olds as measured by national assessments in 1969, 1973, and 1977." This is probably true. We can't say more than "probably" because the National Assessment of Educational Progress (NAEP) was not initially designed to provide longitudinal data, in spite of the presence of the word *progress* in its name. In 1977, NAEP officials decided that such trend data would be useful, and the 1973 and 1969 results were recalculated using only the items those two assessments had in common with the 1977 assessment. Thus the data points the commissioners saw were backward extrapolations in time using only some of the data that had been collected in 1969 and 1973.

Beyond that, and more important, we should ask why the commissioners selected only science and why they selected only seventeen-year-olds to make their point. NAEP also tests nine- and thirteen-year-olds. NAEP also tests reading and mathematics at those three ages. So if the decline is widespread and awful, why weren't the other ages and other subjects included?

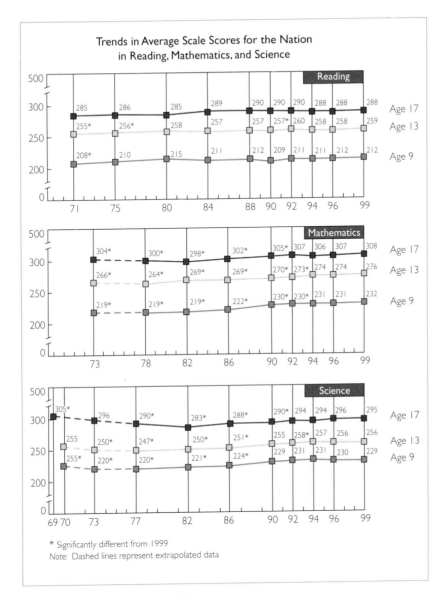

FIG. 2 Trends in Reading, Math, and Science

If we look at all nine trend lines (three subjects tested at three different ages), as shown in Figure 2, we quickly see that the science trend for seventeen-year-olds is the *only* one that shows a "steady decline."[3] It is the only one that will support the report's crisis rhetoric and it was the only one mentioned. (Terrel Bell, the secretary of education who commissioned *A Nation at Risk,* was quite candid in his memoir *The Thirteenth Man* about how he had heard many stories about the terrible state of public schools and had convened the commission to document the stories.)

Another indicator of our low estate from *A Nation at Risk:* "Average achievement of high school students on most standardized tests is now lower than 26 years ago when Sputnik was launched." The commission didn't even *have* data from "most standardized tests" because most standardized tests did not permit trend analysis over such a long period as twenty-six years. Only one did, the Iowa Tests of Educational Development, or ITED (the Iowa Tests of Basic Skills also permit such trend analysis, but the ITBS are given in grades 3–8 and the statement mentions only high schools). By Iowa law, each new form of these tests, first published in 1927, must be equated to the previous form. Such equating permits comparisons over time.

Figure 3 shows the trends for the national normings of the ITBS (norming is explained on pages 121–123). Tests are renormed every five to seven years. Data from Iowa, collected each year, indicate a decline in test scores from 1965 to 1975 and then strong upward trends. These results and the causes of the decline are discussed on pages 34 to 35.

For the ITED, the lower-than-Sputnik statement was true, but only partially representative: test scores had fallen, but when the commission was looking at them, they had risen for five consecutive years, something the commission didn't bother to report. The statement was not true for the ITBS, which provided data from grades 3 through 8; those scores were higher than they were when Sputnik first orbited the earth.

As noted earlier, a lack of specificity is a common flaw in statistical statements. The commission failed to specify the statistics in some of its examples: "Some 23 million American adults are functionally illiterate by the simplest tests of everyday reading, writing, and comprehension." And just

---

3. There are newer data, but the collection of science trend data has been terminated. In addition, the most important data points are those of the 1970s—the commissioners were meeting and looking at the trends in 1982. For the record, the 2004 data for math showed gains. Gains were also found in reading for nine-year-olds.

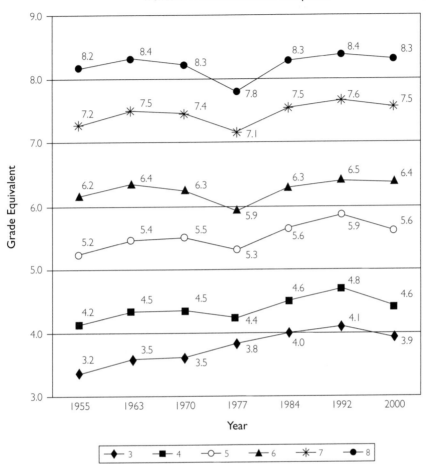

Trends in ITBS Achievement Composite

Grade equivalents referenced to national norms

FIG. 3 National Norming Test Results

what is "functionally illiterate"? It is one of the most slippery concepts ever put forth in education. Early in the twentieth century, you were functionally literate if you could sign your name. Later, functional literacy was defined as having attended school through at least the third grade. Thankfully, researchers in literacy have stopped using the term, although it still finds favor among some school critics.

Note that the tests of reading, writing, and comprehension are not specified beyond being the "simplest" and "everyday"—whatever that means. Vague terms like these might be passable for everyday conversation, but they don't cut it in research.

> **Principle of Data Interpretation:** *Look for and beware of selectivity in the data.*

If an assertion focuses on a limited range of data (say, science for seventeen-year-olds) when it could be expanded to other data (science, math, and reading for nine-, thirteen-, and seventeen-year-olds), ask yourself why the authors don't provide that other data. Ask, What would they lose by showing it all? Then go look for yourself at what the missing data show.

We can refer to overcoming selectivity as Finding the Little Numbers That Aren't There. For instance, in the spring of 2005 the Achievement Alliance published a newsletter that claimed great success for an elementary school it claimed had previously been known as the worst elementary school in the city (which we won't name). Now I have to confess that my skeptic's hat was already on before I read about this school because of who sponsors the Achievement Alliance: the Education Trust, the Business Roundtable, the National Center for Educational Accountability, the Citizens' Commission on Civil Rights, and the National Council of La Raza. I have no experience with La Raza, but the research I have seen from the Citizens' Commission has been weak, and I don't trust the other three organizations at all.

The summary blurb for this school said, "At [this elementary school] African American and Hmong students outscore white students in math." This is a flat assertion and it was not true.

The test in question is scored on a five-point scale with at least a 3 necessary to meet state standards. A higher proportion of African American third graders did meet the state standards of a 3 or better, but their actual *score* was lower than that of the white group. This happened because, while the African American students scored at levels 3 and 4, none of them scored at the highest level, level 5. A substantial proportion of white students attained a 5. And the *proportion of students* at a given *level of achievement* is not a *score.*

To distinguish between a proportion of students at a certain level of achievement and their test scores is not to split hairs. It is an important difference and, unfortunately, a difference not realized in all too many instances. For example, the usually excellent *New York Times* education columnist Michael Winerip confused the two in his June 29, 2005, article titled

"Test Scores Are Up, So Why Isn't Everybody Happy?" The distinction and its importance are discussed on pages 52–58.

No one should detract from the fact that a large portion of these African American kids—80 percent—scored 3 or better nor from the fact that these kids scored much better than African American students statewide. On the other hand, think about the Little Numbers That Aren't There: The school is a K–6 school and the state in question also tests children in the fifth grade and tests in reading as well as math, but the newsletter reported no scores for fifth graders, nor did it report any data for reading. Why not?

Well, when I went to the state department of education's website for the school, I found that the fifth-grade data did not support the summary statement. Neither did the data for reading. The African American third graders at the school substantially outscored African Americans statewide, but at the fifth grade, their reading scores were lower than those for African Americans across the state.

It would be sufficient, and sounder, to simply celebrate the achievement of the African American third graders and to hope that they would hang on to their achievement as they moved through the later grades. But to hype the school and to fail to present the full picture that the complete data paint is to destroy the credibility of both the school's accomplishments and the organizations involved. It is to indulge in propaganda, not truth telling.

This principle of watching out for selectivity will sometimes have to be used in conjunction with Show Me the Data! *A Nation at Risk* did not reveal that the lower-than-Sputnik test scores were from the Iowa Tests of Educational Development, and many people would not know that just from reading the booklet. So you'd have to ask the commissioners or, more likely, one of the people in the U.S. Department of Education who served as staff to the commission.

Selecting the "right" data is akin to selecting the "right" words in a movie review. Of the generally panned *Must Love Dogs,* one critic wrote, "Such great performances . . . such a dreadful movie." One could expect newspaper ads for the movie to herald "Great performances!"

Throwing Readers Off the Scent with Rhetoric

Pay attention to the numbers in a report and to the rhetoric surrounding them. They don't always match. For instance, for almost a quarter of a century, educational consultant and self-described "radical" Denis Doyle has tried to portray American public school teachers as hypocrites, claiming that they teach in public schools but send their own children to private schools. Doyle's own analyses though—using census data from 1980, 1990, and 2000—don't support his claim.

You sure wouldn't know that from the rhetoric. Doyle (1995) sets up teachers by calling them "connoisseurs" of education. That makes them knowledgeable enough to keep their kids out of public schools. "Not to make too fine a point, teachers . . . know how to address the nation's education crisis: they vote with their feet and their pocketbooks. They choose private schools for their children when they think it serves their needs." Well of course! All parents who choose private schools think such schools serve their needs. So what? Note, too, the rhetorical flourish about "the nation's education crisis." The crisis is not described, but merely assumed. The reader is expected to take it for granted.

Doyle continues: "If private schools are good enough for public school teachers, why aren't they good enough for poor children?" In the field of logic, this is known as a *non sequitur*, meaning "it doesn't follow." There is no logical connection between the first half of the question and the second half.

But there's more: "With teachers choosing private schools, the truth is self-evident: while they work in public schools they choose private schools for their own children because they believe they are better." So, suddenly, the rhetoric implies that all public school teachers, whom he has earlier defined as connoisseurs, are also Benedict Arnolds.

But when Doyle actually gets around to showing the numbers, they look like this (Doyle, Diepold, and Deschryver 2004):

Percent of Public School Teachers and General
Public with Children in Private Schools

	Teachers	General Public
1990	12.1	13.1
2000	10.6	12.1

Note that between 1990 and 2000, despite the constant carping by critics, charter school promoters, and voucher advocates about the low quality of public schools, the proportion of both public school teachers and the general public with children in private schools dropped. Actually, these numbers, which came from a report by the Census Bureau, are not complete, although the complete numbers don't lead to a different conclusion. It will come as no surprise to readers to realize that, for a variety of reasons, some families send their kids to *both* public and private schools. If we remove these from the count for 2000 then 9.4 percent of the general public and 7.9 percent of public school teachers used private schools exclusively.

Obviously, if you compare two groups on a given set of data, those two groups should be comparable. But to compare teachers with the general public is to compare noncomparable groups. Over 20 percent of the "general public" lives in poverty, defined in 2005 as an annual income of $19,350 or less for a family of four. Many private schools' tuition these days exceeds $20,000 per year, and even the more reasonable tuitions at religious schools would exclude most of the poor unless they received some outside assistance such as a school-sponsored or privately sponsored scholarship or public or private voucher.

We don't pay teachers princely sums, but they do earn, on average, two and a half times what a family of four in poverty earns. And they are often not the sole wage earner in a family. Since the tendency to use private schools increases with increasing income, it becomes even more remarkable to see fewer teachers using private schools than the general public.

> **Principle of Data Interpretation:** *When comparing groups, make sure the groups are comparable.*

Once again, I need to add that statistics are often more complicated than they seem at first glance. For example, we saw above that some teachers send children to both public schools and private schools. The Census Bureau doesn't provide the reason, but one can imagine private schools being used for special needs kids. Some parents probably feel that the private schools, which are generally smaller with smaller classes, would better serve a child the parents perceive as gifted. Or, in many areas, public high schools have more comprehensive curricula, better lab equipment, and more cocurricular activities, and parents might avail themselves of this while maintaining a child in a private elementary school.

That people, including public school teachers, make use of private schools doesn't imply they reject public schools. If it did, we would have to say that private school teachers reject private schools: Doyle's data show that *fewer than one-third of private school teachers* send their children to private schools.

> **Principle of Data Interpretation:** *Be sure the rhetoric and the numbers match. In all too many instances, they don't.*

Readers might be familiar with a statistic claiming that about 50 percent of public school teachers use private schools. This is a case of what Joel Best called mutant statistics. *Washington Post* pundit George Will closed his March 7, 1993, column with "About half the Chicago public school teachers with school-age children send them to private schools" (1993c, C7). This was true. Will could have pointed out that religion appeared to be the deciding factor in many instances—80 percent of the teachers who used private schools sent their kids to parochial schools—but, narrowly speaking, the claim was right. Doyle had reported that 46 percent of the public school teachers in Chicago used private schools for their own kids. It was the highest rate in the nation.

It took five months of flopping around in Will's brain for this statistic to mutate, and his office never explained to me how it happened, but Will's column of August 26, 1993, claimed that "nationally about half of urban public school teachers with school-age children send their children to private schools" (1993b, A27). Will had conveniently changed the statistic's DNA from Chicago public schools to the nation's urban public schools.

It wasn't true, of course. Digging through the data, I ended up writing an *Education Week* commentary piece, "George Will's Urban Legend" (Bracey 1993, 29). But people continued and continue to use the "about half" figure. For example, an editorial in the *Florida Times-Union* five years later began, "Here's a Jeopardy-type puzzle: the president, the vice president, half the U.S. Senate, a third of the House, and about 40% of the public school teachers. The question is, who sends their children to private schools?" (1998, A10).

> **Principle of Data Interpretation:** *Beware of convenient claims that, whatever the calamity, public schools are to blame.*

A Nation at Risk argued that its indicators of decline compelled us to dedicate ourselves to the reform of our educational system. Did they?

Figure 4 shows the results of the Iowa Tests of Basic Skills over time. These results are for Iowa because data are collected there annually, producing smooth curves (the data from national studies arrive every five to seven

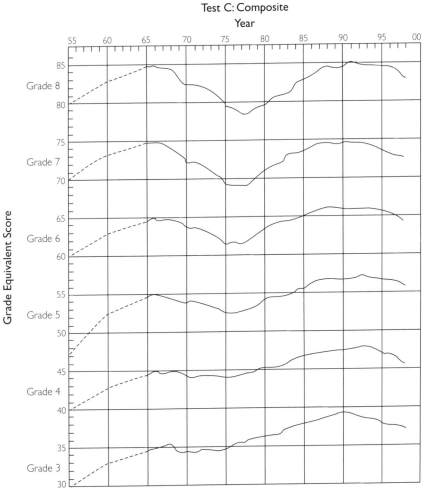

Test C: Composite

Grade equivalents referenced to Iowa's norms

FIG. 4 Trends for Iowa Tests of Basic Skills

years). A glance back to Figure 3, though, will show the comparability of Iowa and national data in terms of *trends*. The scores cannot be directly compared because national scores are referenced to national norms and Iowa scores are referenced to Iowa norms. Iowa students outscore the nation generally, which leads to them have tougher norms. That is, an average score within Iowa is an above average score when compared with the nation as a whole.

The Iowa tests have existed since the 1920s but in 1955 underwent such a massive revision that the developers decided to call 1955 year zero and to track changes from there. As we can see, scores rise from 1955 to about 1965, then fall for a decade, and then reverse direction and rise again to *record high levels* (why wasn't this news?).

So there really was a test score decline. Had the schools gone awry?

Consider the falling test scores in the broader social context. In 1965, we were just coming out of the "togetherness" years of the Eisenhower administration (1952–60). Among the most popular television shows was *The Adventures of Ozzie and Harriet* (1953–66). *Washington Post* columnist George Will (2001) argued you could see the '60s coming in the '50s in people such as Holden Caulfied in *Catcher in the Rye* (1951), Sidney Poitier in *The Blackboard Jungle* (1955), James Dean in *Rebel Without a Cause* (1955), and Marlon Brando in *The Wild One* (1953) (B7).

But Will didn't make his "prediction" until 2001. The '50s and early '60s were much more dominated by conformity and anonymity, as described in *The Lonely Crowd* (1950), *The Man in the Gray Flannel Suit* (1955), *The Organization Man* (1956), and *A Nation of Sheep* (1961).

By contrast, 1965 was a year after James Chaney, Michael Schwerner, and Andrew Goodman were murdered in Mississippi while trying to register black voters. It was a year after the Civil Rights Act of 1964 and a year after the Free Speech Movement had exploded into the streets at the University of California, Berkeley. It was the year of the Watts riots in Los Angeles, after which urban violence swept across the nation.

The decade of the test-score decline was the decade of acid rock, of Woodstock and Altamont, the summer of love, the Beatles, the Stones, Jefferson Airplane, psychedelic posters and psychedelic drugs, and *The Electric Kool-Aid Acid Test* (both the trip itself and the book). People seeking social change formed Students for a Democratic Society, the Weathermen, the Weather Underground, the Student Non-Violent Coordinating Committee, and the Black Panthers, and Patty Hearst was kidnapped by the Symbionese Liberation Army. It was the decade of the "counterculture" and descriptions of it, such as *The Making of a Counter Culture* (1969) and *The Greening of America* (1970). It was a decade where feminism took hold in *The Feminine Mystique* (1963), *Sexual Politics* (1969), and *The Female Eunuch* (1970).

It was the decade when fifty-eight thousand Americans lost their lives in Vietnam while Country Joe and the Fish sang, "Ain't no time to wonder why, whoopee, we're all gonna die." It included Kent State, the Chicago police riot, and Watergate, which led to the resignation of President Richard Nixon in 1974. The decade began barely a year after the assassination of John F.

Kennedy Jr., and it included the assassinations of his brother Robert, Martin Luther King Jr., and Malcolm X.

As for doing well in school, it was the decade of *Teaching as a Subversive Activity* (1969), *The Underachieving School* (1969), *How to Survive in Your Native Land* (1971), *The Student as Nigger* (1962), *Deschooling Society* (1971), *School Is Dead* (1972), and *The Pedagogy of the Oppressed* (1970). Books focused on the inadequate schools of poor children included *Death at an Early Age* (1967), *36 Children* (1967), and *The Way It Spozed to Be* (1968).

Aside from the Reconstruction period following the Civil War, the decade of falling test scores was likely the most socially volatile in the nation's history. It would have been a bloody *miracle* if test scores *hadn't* fallen.

This little psychosociological minitreatise is neither pure distraction nor an explanation limited to one phenomenon, a drop in test scores. It should lead you to explore the social context of any change in schools. The public schools do not exist in a vacuum. This discussion also leads to another principle.

> **Principle of Data Interpretation:** *Beware of simple explanations for complex phenomena.*

As H. L. Mencken (n.d.) once said, "For every complex problem there is an answer that is clear, simple and wrong." Other abuses to watch for will pop up in other discussions throughout the book. We turn now to a general examination of the generators of data, variables.

2

The Nature of Variables

What Are Variables?

It is not facetious to say that variables are things that vary, but it is wrong. Some variables are immutable qualities that clump people into categories: gender, ethnicity, age (at a given point in time, anyway).

Otherwise, variables *are* things that vary:

test scores

attendance rates—teacher, student

classroom disruptions

ethnic mixture in a school

socioeconomic mixture in a school

height

weight

dropout rate

teacher turnover rate

distance between pupils of the eyes

slope of the forehead

Obviously, some of these variables have more relevance for education than others. And some are subject to varying definitions. Take socioeconomic mix, for example. This is often defined simply as the percent of students eligible for free and reduced-price lunches. This is not a particularly precise measure, but it is often the only one handily available to estimate poverty rates and has to serve as a proxy for a true measure. However, students living in families that earn up to 185 percent of the poverty level are eligible for these lunches. There are probably differences between schools where most families are close to the official poverty level of $19,350 a year for a family of four and schools where most families are near the 185 percent limit, which is almost $36,000 a year.

This statistic is not usually used at the high school level because teenagers do not like to admit to poverty (some schools now have "smart cards," which, when inserted into a slot, subtract the appropriate amount for a meal, preventing anyone else from knowing how much any particular student paid).

Principal Variables of Concern Under the No Child Left Behind Law

grade

ethnicity

special education status

free and reduced-price meal eligibility

English language learner status

percent of students taking the test

math scores

reading scores

science scores (starting in 2007)

percent of "proficient" students

percent of high school graduates

percent of "highly qualified" teachers

adequate yearly progress

Adequate yearly progress is included because, while it is constant for some states, for most states the amount called for in the state plan varies from year to year.

Other Variables Commonly Considered in Studies of Schools

Demographic Variables

enrollment by grade level

ethnic composition

student mobility rate

percent of limited English proficient students

percent of special education students

parent income levels

economic base

unemployment rate

Student Variables

grade point averages

test scores

percent of students taking college admissions tests

scores of students taking college admissions tests

percent of students taking Advanced Placement tests or IB examinations

scores of students taking Advanced Placement tests or IB examinations

number of Advanced Placement tests taken per student

percent of students showing "AP mastery" (a category defined by the College Board) percent of eighth graders taking algebra

percent of students enrolling in

> four-year institutions of higher education
>
> two-year institutions of higher education
>
> other postsecondary educational programs

percent of students meeting state standards

dropout rate

graduation rate

promotion rate

retention-in-grade rate

tardy rate

truancy rate

expulsion rate

participation in cocurricular programs

percent of seniors obtaining honors, regular, or special diplomas

student surveys (of former as well as current students)

changes over time in all of the above variables

Obviously, not all of these variables are independent of each other. As the promotion rate rises, the retention-in-grade rate falls. As the retention-in-grade rate rises, the dropout rate also likely rises and the graduation rate falls. Some of the variables carry political baggage: schools with low retention-in-grade rates might be vulnerable to the charge of social promotion or promotion based on seat time. The charge is often inaccurate because students who are perceived as having trouble are often identified and given extra attention before promotion. It might be wise, though, for a school to utilize another variable in connection with promotion or retention rates: the number of special programs (tutoring, after school, Saturday, summer, at home online) available to students having academic difficulties.

Similarly, there might well be an inverse relationship between the percent taking AP tests and the scores on AP tests. Jay Mathews, an education writer for the *Washington Post,* contends that it is the AP experience that is important, not necessarily the score on the test. It's important, he feels, that students experience the challenge of an AP course and test. Some schools agree with Mathews, and they score high on his Challenge Index, which is the number of AP exams taken divided by the size of the senior class. If in a school there are one hundred seniors and two hundred AP tests are taken, that school's Challenge Index is 2. Mathews considers any value of the index above 1 to be healthy.

Some schools don't agree with Mathews, or maybe they think high scores are more important, PR-wise, than a high participation rate. They discourage students they think won't do well from taking AP courses or, if they permit these students in the courses, discourage them from taking the tests. This probably increases the school's average AP score. Whichever way a school goes will depend on its philosophy and, on occasion, which variable the principal feels is the better variable to brag about to the board and the press.

Variables are what we use to generate statistics. In the second paragraph of this book, I noted that statistics are collected for a purpose. It could be a good purpose or a devious one. The point is that variables are not pure indications that reveal their meaning to us immediately. They must be interpreted.

Teacher Variables

percentage of teachers with major or minor in teaching area

percentage of teachers holding regular certification

teacher experience

teacher turnover rate

> overall

> in first five years of teaching

teacher attendance rate

retirement projections

number and use of support staff

how variables used for one building differ from district/state averages/
rates

The number of variables listed might seem overwhelming, since many of
them can interact in complex ways. To manipulate many variables at once is
beyond human ken, and people have turned to computer programs and the
concept of data warehousing and "data mining." A warehouse holds a lot of
data, and computer programs mine the data in sophisticated ways. The state
of this art in education is, at present, quite primitive, but it will surely get
more sophisticated.

According to Streifer, engineers have developed computer technologies
known as neural nets that can answer questions that are asked in natural
language (as opposed to keywords used by search engines or in a program-
ming language like C or JavaScript). One such net was asked, "What baseball games were played in the continental United States during May 2001
where the temperature was between 60 and 70 degrees Fahrenheit?"
(Streifer 2004, 33). I have no idea *why* this question was asked, but the system went onto the Internet, compiled a list of all games played in May and
compared the results with weather reports at the time the games were
played. This is like asking, "What is the effect of student mobility on
achievement?" and having the computer find all of the correct data, sort and
analyze them, and provide an answer. Won't happen soon.

Indeed, only a few states and districts currently have the computer
power to track students over time throughout the system. I think Arizona
was the first state to be able to find a student wherever that student was as
long as the student was in the Arizona public school system. When I worked
in a school district in the late 1980s, while the district was affluent and sophisticated, the database that held test scores was unconnected to other da-
tabases. Asking a question like, "What is the relationship between test
scores in the first three grades and dropping out?" wasn't even possible.
Many school computer systems in those days contained mostly budget and
personnel data. The finance and personnel computer systems were much
more extensive than those for examining the performance of the school system in terms of the academic variables listed earlier.

The onset of No Child Left Behind (NCLB), though, with its massive
record-keeping requirements, has resulted in a number of states developing
student tracking systems.

Measures of Central Tendency:
How Mean Is the Median?

Without averages, the media might collapse. The average American gets 7 hours of sleep, eats 24 pounds of butter a year, drinks more beer than wine, weighs 260 pounds, and earns $22,000 a year. These are all fake figures, of course, but you get the idea. The average American probably reads or hears the word *average* ten or more times a day. It's the all-American statistic.

When George W. Bush was stumping for his first round of tax cuts, he claimed the average worker would enjoy a break of, let's say, $1,500. Opponents of the cuts harrumphed that the average tax break would be more like $150. Who was right?

Both Bush and his critics were right. They just used different statistics to define average. Bush appropriated the mean; his critics relied on the median. And while both were "right," in this case the median was the more representative, more meaningful statistic. To see why, let's say the following distribution of numbers represents the wealth of eleven people.

1. $10,000

2. $10,000 mode

3. $10,000

4. $20,000

5. $20,000

6. $40,000 median

7. $60,000

8. $60,000

9. $70,000

10. $80,000

11. $65,000,000,000

mean = $5,909,125,455

To calculate the average—that is, the mean—we add all the numbers and divide by the number of numbers. If you had twenty-five students in your class and you wanted to know the mean percent correct on a test, you would take each student's individual percent correct, add all of these individual students' scores together, and then divide by twenty-five.

In the list above, adding all of these numbers up and dividing by eleven gives us a mean of $5,909,125,455—an average wealth of almost $6 billion. The mean is more than $5 billion even though only one person is worth more than $80,000. That one rich guy was not randomly chosen. The amount listed as number 11 was Bill Gates' approximate wealth in March 2005 (Gates' changing fortunes—he had dropped $5 billion by mid October—can be seen at http://philip.greenspun.com/WealthClock).

This example makes an important point: Extreme values affect the mean. In Bush's plan, wealthy people got a much larger tax break in terms of dollar amount than you and I, and those extreme values pushed the average (mean) up.

Bush's critics chose another measure of average, the median. The median is the number that divides a group into equal halves. In the previous list, the median is $40,000; half of the people are worth more and half are worth less. And since we are just counting people to find the midway point in the distribution, not taking their wealth into account, Bill Gates is just another guy.

Bush's critics showed that most people would get much less of a break than Bush claimed because Bush's program favored the wealthy and that would skew the "average" using the mean as the statistic. An analysis by the *Washington Post* revealed that teachers would get about enough to buy a new TV, while someone making $1,000,000 a year would get a tax break about twice as large as the average teacher's annual salary.

That table in the *Post* showed me doing better than teachers. I got a break equal to the price of a forty-nine-inch big-screen TV, about $1,500 at the time. A person making a million dollars a year got a $90,000 break. If we added five people who got a $1,000 break and four who got a $2,000 break with my break and the rich guy's break, the mean break for these eleven people would be $9,500, but the median would be less than one-sixth of that, $1,500. No wonder Bush went with the mean.

Tax Break

$1,000

$1,000

$1,000

$1,000

$1,000

$1,500

$2,000

$2,000

$2,000

$2,000

$90,000

mean = $9,500

median = $1,500

People often calculate both the mean and the median and then choose to use whichever one best supports whatever point they're trying to make.

There is a third statistic for indicating average, called the *mode*. The mode is simply the most frequently occurring number. In the first list above, the mode is $10,000, and in the second, it is $1,000. The mode is not used nearly as often as the mean and the median. It will convey a sense of the shape of the distribution in sentences like "The distribution is bimodal." This sentence almost applies to the second list, as there are almost as many $2,000 tax breaks as $1,000 breaks. Calling a distribution bimodal tells the reader or listener that if the distribution were graphed, it would have two humps.

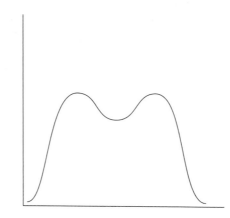

A Bimodal Distribution

> Principle of Data Interpretation: *Make certain you know what statistic is being used when someone is talking about the "average."*

Although the lists above were contrived to make the three measures have different values, that sometimes happens in real life, too. And it's useful to have all three measures to give a complete picture of what "average" looks like. Technically the three measures are referred to as *measures of central tendency*. For reasons unknown to me, the word *mean* was long ago replaced by the symbol $\overline{X}$, pronounced, "X-bar."

In the June 29, 2005, edition of the *Virginian Pilot* (metro Norfolk), an article appeared titled, "Some Teachers Practicing Zero Intolerance." Teachers in Norfolk and Virginia Beach, it seems, have developed an intolerance for giving zeros to students even for work not handed in because the zero has too much of an impact on students' overall grades. That is because the teachers are calculating the average grade using the mean and a zero is an outlier, a bit like Bill Gates' wealth.

The solution, potentially, is to use the median, not the mean. If a student had received grades of, say, 0, 65, 65, 70, 75, 75, and 80, the mean comes out at 61 even, though only one of seven grades falls below that figure. I suppose some moralists might say, "It would teach him a lesson," but a fairer approach might be to use the median. The median of the given distribution is 70, a figure more representative of the student's work, but still taking the 0 into account.

If the distribution of scores is "normal"—that is, looks like the familiar bell curve—all three measures of central tendency will be identical. In fact, if the mean, median, and mode are *different*, you know, without looking at the distribution, that it is not normal, although it could be close to normal if the three measures are close. This can be important because many other statistics *presume* a bell-shaped distribution, and if it isn't shaped that way, these statistics might not give accurate information.

To summarize:

To find the mean: Add all of the numbers together and divide by the number of numbers.

To find the median: Find the number that divides the group such that half of the group score higher than that number and half score lower.

To find the mode: Find the most frequently occurring number.

Populations and Samples

Most of the time, our statistics come from a sample of all possible people who could provide them. To really know how well our fourth graders read, we should test all 4 million of them (presuming we have a reading test that is fair to all 4 million). Then we would say we tested the *population* of fourth graders. That would be ever so expensive, so instead we test a sample. In order to be comfortable that our statistics about reading proficiency lead to the proper inferences, we have to know something about how the sample was gathered. Was it a *representative* sample, or a *biased* sample? If we're measuring height and we find that the average male in our sample stands six feet six inches tall, it is one thing if the group is a representative sample of all men and quite another thing if the sample was made up only of basketball players.

Biased samples can have enormous consequences for research-based decision making. The highly regarded *Literary Digest* had successfully predicted every presidential election from 1916 through 1932 by mailing out postcards that looked like ballots and having people return them filled in. In 1936, it added names from automobile registrations and telephone directories and conducted the largest poll ever, sending "ballots" to more than 10 million people and getting back 2.4 million completed forms.

The *Digest* confidently predicted Alf Landon in a landslide over Franklin D. Roosevelt. Alas for them, the *Literary Digest*'s editors did not realize they had used a biased sample: not only were cars the province of the well-off, but in 1936 only one in four households had telephones, so a phone, too, was something of a status symbol.

During the first years of the Great Depression, voting had shifted along class lines: the poor and working class had come to vote for Democrats, the more affluent for Republicans. The *Literary Digest*'s poll missed a lot of Democratic homes that didn't have telephones. Even a sample of 2.4 million people can lead to the wrong conclusion if the sample doesn't represent the population from which it is drawn. The *Literary Digest* folded shortly after the election.

Here's a homely example about populations and samples derived from an image in Huff's *How to Lie with Statistics* (1954). Suppose you wanted to judge the quality of corn in a field of corn with about one thousand ears of corn. The whole field is the population of corn because you aren't concerned with anything except this one field of corn. If you picked five ears, you'd have a small sample, and judging the whole field might be iffy. If you walked randomly around the field and picked fifty ears, you'd be more confident about your judgment, and if you picked one hundred ears, you'd be more confident still.

If you had walked in only one-quarter of the field and sampled fifty ears, you might be less confident. You still have fifty ears, but you haven't touched three-quarters of the field. If part of that remaining three-quarters was in the shade a lot of the day, its corn might be different. Or if half the field was on a slope, the corn might be different because it would get less water—rains would run off more rapidly.

We'll talk more about samples later.

Measures of Dispersion

An average tells us something about the group, and this can be important information. We also need to know something about how the individuals in the group vary. In the previous example about wealth, people varied in wealth from $10,000 to $80,000, except for that one exceptional person.

To say that people varied in wealth from $10,000 to $80,000 is to almost calculate one measure of dispersion, the *range*. The range for these ten people would be $70,000; to get the range you subtract the lowest amount from the highest. Of course, if we include Bill Gates, the range goes out to $65 billion. This reveals an important limitation of the range: like the mean, the range is affected by extreme values.

The most common measure of how scores are dispersed around the average is the *standard deviation*. A standard deviation is a mathematical concept—for a long time it was called the root mean square error, a mathematical mouthful—but it can be understood conceptually without reference to mathematics.

The standard deviation provides information about how much scores vary around the mean. A large standard deviation means that scores vary a lot, while a small standard deviation indicates they are more tightly bunched close to the mean. In education and psychology, it is used almost exclusively with normal, bell-shaped distributions. Its calculation involves the mean, but recall that in a normal distribution, the mean, median, and mode are identical, so a calculation using median or mode would generate the same number.

Take a look at the two curves in Figure 5. Both of these are bell shaped, but for one the scores range out much farther from the average than in the

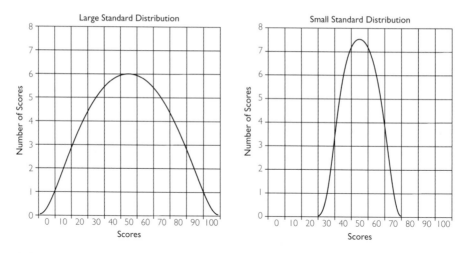

FIG. 5   Two Normal Distributions

other. The standard deviation of the first would be larger than the standard deviation of the second.

People use the standard deviation largely because it has useful properties that other measures of dispersion do not. Principally, if you know the average and the standard deviation of a distribution and the score of a particular person, you know how that person compares in rank with everyone else in the distribution.

That is because, in a normal distribution, no matter the *size* of the standard deviation, the *proportion* of all people contained in an SD, as standard deviations are usually referred to, is invariant: 34 percent of all people will score between the average and one standard deviation away from the mean. Another 14 percent will score between one and two standard deviations away from the mean. And another 2 percent will score between two and three standard deviations away from the mean (these numbers are rounded, and the mathematically inclined can find the exact figures in Klugh 1986, 56).

Thus, a person or a score that is +1.0 SD above the mean scores better than 84 percent of the people or scores in the distribution: the 34 percent between the mean and +1.0 SD and the 50 percent below the mean.

Mathematically, the tails of the normal curve go on forever, but practically, virtually every score will be found between −3.0 SD and +3.0 SD. (See Figure 6.)

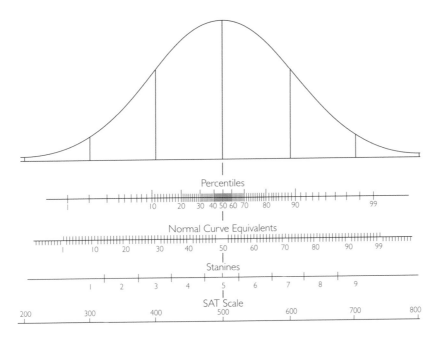

Percentiles

Normal Curve Equivalents

Stanines

SAT Scale

FIG. 6 Normal Curve

Not all distributions are perfectly normal. Sometimes scores will bunch up at the high end or the low end of the range. Such distributions are called skewed distributions. A distribution in which there are few scores at the negative end is called a negatively skewed distribution, and one in which scores pile up at the negative end is called a positively skewed distribution. This is exactly opposite of how most of us would expect them to be named when we look at the curves. (See Figure 7.) The standard deviation loses much of its meaning in skewed distributions

Is the Normal Curve a No-No in Education?

Now, a number of people have argued that the normal curve is antithetical to education. Benjamin Bloom, creator of the Taxonomy of Educational Objectives, was particularly disdainful:

> There is nothing sacred about the normal curve. It is the distribution most appropriate to chance and random activity. Education is a purposeful activity, and we seek to have the students learn what

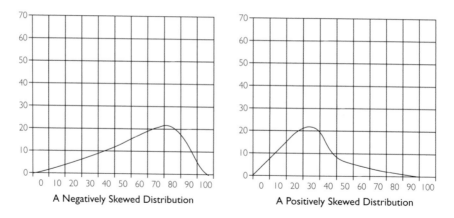

A Negatively Skewed Distribution   A Positively Skewed Distribution

FIG. 7 Two Skewed Distribution

we teach. If we are effective in our instruction, the distribution of achievement should be very different from the normal curve. In fact, we may even insist that our educational efforts have been *unsuccessful* to the extent that the distribution of achievement approximates the normal curve. (Bloom, Madaus, and Hastings 1981, 52–53)

Bloom had earlier argued that "theoretically, almost all the students can learn to a relatively high level anything the schools have to teach" (1971, 48). For Bloom, the appropriate distribution of achievement in schools is not the normal curve, but the J curve shown below.

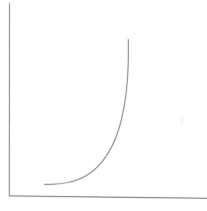

A J Curve

The ideal of the J curve, or perhaps an extremely negatively skewed distribution, evolved into the mantra "all students can learn" and is codified in the No Child Left Behind law, which requires that 100 percent of students be "proficient" in reading, mathematics, and science by the year 2014.[1] Proficient is in quotes because currently each state uniquely defines proficiency.

The principal, but not the only, weakness of both "all children can learn" and NCLB is that both assume that the schools can do it alone. Indeed, NCLB *requires* that the schools do it alone. It ignores the impact of the preschool years and the first two years of school as well as parents, family, and community.

Bloom was rebutting a popular, if erroneous, interpretation of the Coleman report (Coleman 1966). That interpretation was "it's all family." That is, schools don't matter. By this interpretation, the Coleman report found that outside of the contributions to achievement by family and community variables, schools showed only small differences in their contribution to achievement.

Actually, Coleman observed that schools mattered a great deal. He *assumed* the existence of schools and then failed to find large differences *among* schools that were not due to family and community differences. This is quite different than claiming that schools don't matter, which Coleman never did. And, of course, the stated goal of NCLB is to wipe out the impact of those family and community variables—to close the achievement gap between rich and poor, majority and minority. It won't happen, if only because children, from birth to age eighteen, spend only 9 percent of their lives in school.

We might paraphrase Bloom to say that the normal curve is the distribution we often see before any intervention, educational or otherwise. The extent to which education can shift a normal distribution toward a J-curve distribution remains an open question and probably dependent on the situation.

Hypothetical experiment: One fall we have all eighth graders run a mile. The result would probably form a normal curve, with a few children with muscular disabilities lagging with very slow times or not able to complete the task. Then over the school year, we put the eighth grades though a substantial program of physical fitness to build up endurance, leg muscles, and so on. In the spring, we have the students run a mile again.

1. Theoretically, the curve could still be normal, but all scores would have to be to the right of the point that separates "proficient" from "left behind."

What would the springtime distribution of running times look like? Certainly the distribution would have shifted such that the students ran the mile much faster than in the fall. But would the spring distribution still be normal? It's an open question.

What if we gave the slower runners extra training? That is the theory of Bloom's Mastery Learning: give those who are having difficulty extra time to learn. This is what often happens in schools today—children who fail, say, a high school exit examination spend extra time on material reflecting the test's objectives and are given extra help to get them past the hurdle.

Bloom and some of his followers referred to the extra time as a gift that allowed slower students to catch up. This has always seemed to me an acutely "adultocentric" viewpoint. Adults call it a gift. Do the children? It seems plausible to me that if I'm a student having trouble with some schoolwork, the last thing in the world I want to do is spend more time on it.

Giving more time has also been presented as one way of eliminating the achievement gap. It probably doesn't overall because while the slower students are learning material for the exam, those who have already passed have gone on to what Bloom called "enrichment."

Such an approach probably *widens* the achievement gap. In order to understand this, we have to think about two principles of data interpretation in educational research:

> **Principle of Data Interpretation:** *Be aware of whether you are dealing with* **rates** *or* **numbers***. Similarly, be aware of whether you are dealing with* **rates** *or* **scores***.*

Scores are a particular case of numbers, but one that within education requires special attention. But let's start with the more general instance first: rates versus numbers. We often hear that the fastest-growing jobs today are all high-tech, high-skill or that the fastest-growing jobs are in information technology. The phrase *fastest-growing* indicates a rate. It is easiest for something, anything, to be the fastest growing when it is not really very large. If I make one dollar today, two dollars tomorrow, four dollars the next day, and eight dollars the day after that, my *rate* of growth is quite rapid. I'm doubling my income every day. As we saw in the case of the gunned-down children, if

Title	Employment in Thousands		Change %
	2002	**2012**	
Medical Assistant	365	579	59
Network Systems Analyst	186	292	57
Physician's Assistant	63	94	49
Social and Human Services Assistant	305	454	49
Home Health Aide	580	859	48
Medical Records and Health Info Technician	37	54	47
Computer Software Engineer, Applications	394	576	46
Computer Software Engineer, Systems Software	281	409	45
Physical Therapist's Assistant	50	73	45
TOTAL	2,261	**3,390**	

Source: Bureau of Labor Statistics, U.S. Department of Labor

FIG. 8   Ten Fastest-Growing Occupations, 2002–12

that rate keeps up, the *numbers* eventually become very large, but after only four days, the *number* of dollars I've earned is still quite small.

Another example of rates versus numbers: Loudoun County, Virginia, recently replaced Clark County, Nevada (Las Vegas), as the fastest-growing county in the country. But Clark County is about ten times the size of Loudoun. If 20,000 people moved to Loudoun county in a year, its rate of increase would be 10% percent. But if 20,000 move to Vegas, the increase is only 1 percent.

This applies in the area of job growth: The fastest-growing jobs are mostly—but not all—jobs that require high skills and the use of technology. Figure 8 shows the jobs that the Bureau of Labor Statistics (BLS) projects will grow the fastest over the period from 2002 to 2012. It also shows how many of these jobs will exist.

Figure 9 provides the same information but for the occupations that have greatest growth in the *number* of jobs created. One immediately sees that the occupations that will create the most jobs are mostly low-skill, low-paying jobs. A National Public Radio report in the spring of 2005 indicated that the farming industry needs 3 million field workers, a low-pay, low-skill occupation that doesn't even show up in the BLS count.

In this case, as in so many others, the impression given by looking at rates of growth is very different from that given by looking at numbers.

Test scores are a kind of number. Passing rates are, naturally, a kind of rate. But sometimes the rate shows up misleadingly where a number should

Title	Employment in Thousands		Change %
	2002	2012	
Retail Sales	4,076	4,672	15
Cashiers	3,432	3,886	13
Office Clerks, General	2,991	3,301	10
Registered Nurses	2,284	2,908	27
Janitors and Cleaners	2,267	2,681	18
Waiters and Waitresses	2,097	2,464	18
Food Preparers and Servers	1,990	2,444	23
Customer Service Representatives	1,894	2,354	24
Truck and Tractor Drivers	1,767	2,104	19
Postsecondary Teachers	1,581	2,184	38
TOTAL	24,379	28,998	

Source: Bureau of Labor Statistics, U.S. Department of Labor

FIG. 9 Occupations with Largest Numbers of Jobs Created from 2002 to 2012

be. For instance, in *Do Graduation Tests Measure Up?* Michael Cohen and Matt Gandal, president and vice president, respectively, of Achieve, present the curves in Figure 10 and argue that they show a diminishing achievement gap between whites and minorities (Cohen and Gandal 2004). This graph is for the MCAS, but it could as easily be the TAKS, SOL, WASL, CAHSEE, or any such exit exam.[2]

Now, people typically talk about the achievement gap in terms of *scores.* For instance, it is often said, accurately, that the average black twelfth grader scores about the same on the National Assessment of Educational Progress as the average white eighth grader.

But Cohen and Gandal present the achievement gap in terms of *rates.* This is neither logical nor legitimate.

Take a look at the leftmost points on the curves. They show a huge—40 percentage point—gap in passing rates between African Americans and whites the first time the students took the test in grade 10 (37 percent versus 77 percent). The gap for Hispanics versus whites is an even larger 48 points. The tenth-grade test liberated 77 percent of white students to study material

2. MCAS = Massachusetts Comprehensive Assessment System; TAKS = Texas Assessment of Knowledge and Skills; SOL = Standards of Learning (Virginia); WASL = Washington Assessment of Student Learning; CAHSEE = California High School Exit Exam.

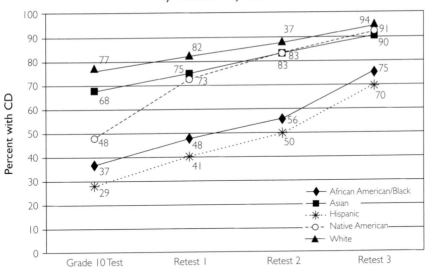

Percent of Students Attaining the Competency Determination by Race/Ethnicity: Class of 2003

FIG. 10   MCAS Results

other than what is covered by the test. Only 37 percent of African American students were similarly freed. One could predict, in fact, that with each re-test, for those who failed, the material that the test covers became more and more of the curriculum. In fact, a story from a teacher in Texas described how each day some of her students were removed from her regular instruction to receive help on the objectives covered by TAKS; these students also missed art, physical education, and library break.

To get an accurate picture of how large the true achievement gap is, one would have to come back in eleventh and twelfth grade and give not just the MCAS, but tests that covered *what had been taught in those grades.* If the test is given in the tenth grade, what happens to the students the next year? Surely the 63 percent of African American students who failed the test in tenth grade did not take algebra II in eleventh grade or solid geometry and trig in twelfth. Seventy-seven percent of the white students, however, were free to take such advanced courses or other courses covering curriculum not on the MCAS. Thus, many white students studied coursework that many black students never had an opportunity to study, thereby increasing the achievement gap.

There is more. We don't know from the Cohen–Gandal graphs what scores the students attained. Let's assume that students needed a score of 60 to pass the MCAS. The average score for whites could have been, let's say, 74, with 23 percent scoring below 60. The average score for blacks could have been 62, with 71 percent scoring below 60. But if the average score for blacks is 62, that means a lot of black students came very close to the passing score of 60. A small improvement in their scores would lead to a large increase in their passing rate, but not necessarily to any gain measured against white students' scores.

Something like the above actually took place in the spring of 2005 in New York, where large gains were reported in the passing rates on the third-grade test. A story in the *New York Times*, though, indicated that many students had scored close to the passing score the previous year. If this year's third graders were similar to last year's—a reasonable assumption with large numbers of students—it would take only a small increase in score to lift them over the bar.

This is apparently what happened. David Herszenhorn, the *Times* reporter who covered the story, indicated by email that the affluent suburbs had seen large gains in scores (this fact should have been in the story and Herszenhorn said that editors cut those paragraphs). Because whites had had such high passing rates on the test previously, their score gains didn't show up as large gains in the passing rate. If you're only reporting passing rates, and the score needed to pass is 60, it doesn't matter whether the average score is 75 or 94.

The two statistics, passing rates and scores, can vary independently. We can see this in a hypothetical situation. Suppose in 2004, 100 percent of whites passed the test and that their average score was 78. Suppose then, in 2005, 100 percent of whites passed the test and that their average score was 92. As long as we're looking only at pass rates—which is what New York City and a lot of states are looking at—we won't see any improvement. The pass rate is 100 percent both times. The average score, though, rises quite a bit from 2004 to 2005.

Continuing with this hypothetical outcome, suppose that in 2004, 40 percent of blacks failed with an average score of 62. Suppose then, in 2005, 30 percent of blacks failed with an average score of 68. Their passing rate and their average score both went up.

But . . . if the scores of white children rose from 78 to 92 and the scores of the black students rose from 62 to 68, the achievement gap *increased*.

White students' scores rose by fourteen points while the average score of blacks rose only six points. The score difference between blacks and whites in 2004 was sixteen points (78 − 62). In 2005 it was twenty-four points (92 − 68).

Here's the experiment in tabular form:

	Pass Rate	Average Score	Gap
Black Students, 2004	60%	62	
			16
White Students, 2004	100%	78	
Black Students, 2005	70%	68	
			24
White Students, 2005	100%	92	
Score Needed to Pass = 60			

In sum, passing rates tell you *nothing* about what is happening to any achievement gap. But it remains quite likely that those who fail an exit exam, or fail to contribute to a school's making adequate yearly progress under NCLB, will spend more time learning the tasks that are on the tests while those who pass go on to learn new material. The achievement gap has increased. We just don't see it because (1) we are reporting only pass rates, not scores, and (2) we don't test everyone on all of the things that have been taught since the first test.

I don't know how often states or localities report how many students are at or above a given level of achievement, but it seems to be the dominant statistic these days. Such statements are also made when results from the National Assessment of Educational Progress are reported. NAEP has three levels of achievement, basic, proficient, and advanced, and one usually reads in the media statements to the effect that "X percent of fourth graders scored proficient or better." The tendency to report "percent scoring at standard" or "proportion of students scoring proficient or better" has no doubt increased since 2002 because that is a principal statistic of No Child Left Behind. Keep in mind, this is some proportion of students that is being referred to; the reference is not to actual scores.

Before leaving the situation in Massachusetts, we need to examine another principle of data interpretation that these data illustrate.

> **Principle of Data Interpretation:** *When comparing either rates or scores over time, make sure the groups remain comparable as the years go by.*

In the spring of 2003, the Massachusetts Department of Education crowed that 93 percent of all students in the class of 2003 had passed the MCAS. And it was true that among the students who were ninth graders in 1999–2000 *and who were still in school in 2003,* 93 percent had passed. But of the 77,733 kids who entered Massachusetts ninth grades, only 60,000 were still around in 2003. The number of those who had passed as a percentage of those who had started out in ninth grade was only 71 percent, not 93 percent. The group of ninth graders has shrunk and is not comparable with the group of twelfth graders four years later.

We don't know what happened to all of those nearly eighteen thousand freshmen who had disappeared from the rolls by the time they were supposed to be seniors. Certainly some had moved to other states and might have passed the test had they remained in Massachusetts. But just as surely, some of them were retained in a grade and were no longer part of the class of 2003, some elected to obtain a GED, and some dropped out of school altogether. Their retention or leaving might well have been triggered by a low score on the MCAS, and had they stayed, they might have continued to fail the test. Using a military analogy, we might call these kids the collateral damage of the test, and, not surprisingly, people who brag about test results don't want to call attention to these kids.

When researcher Anne Wheelock (2004) conducted the appropriate analysis for the class of 2004, which the state boasted had a stellar pass rate of 96 percent, she came up with these numbers:

All students	74%, not 96%
White students	80%, not 98%
African American students	59%, not 88%
Latino students	54%, not 85%
Asian students	89%, not 95%

Each year from ninth grade on, the composition of the class of 2004 had changed and those who had remained in the class of 2004 through twelfth grade were not a representative sample of those who had started as ninth graders.

Rates versus numbers and rates versus scores. They often paint different partial pictures of a situation. You often need to look at both to see the whole picture.

The same is true of *ranks* versus numbers, especially if the numbers in question are scores. If a person ranked at the seventy-third percentile on a test, did that person get a good score? We know that she got a *better* score than 73 percent of those who took the test. But maybe everyone scored low.

In any ranking, while someone gets to rank first, someone *must* rank last. When eight runners flash down the track in the final heat of the men's one-hundred-meter dash in the Olympics, someone will rank eighth, last. He is still the eighth-fastest human being on the planet that day and probably not known to the other runners as Pokey. Similarly, someone who gets a low ranking on the Graduate Record Examination is still among a fairly elite 25 percent—the 25 percent of Americans who have at least a bachelor's degree.

Ranks can also give the appearance that large differences exist among people, schools, districts, states, or nations when, in fact, the differences might be small. This often happens in international studies of reading, mathematics, and science. When American eighth graders finished nineteenth in science among the forty-one nations in the Third International Mathematics and Science Study, the media labeled their performance "mediocre." *Mediocre* was used in place of *average*, but mediocre is a judgment while average is a statistic. In our Olympic race example, the person who finished fourth, average, was probably not referred to as mediocre. In order to properly judge a rank, you need to know something about the context in which it occurs.

Figure 11 shows the ranks of the eighth graders from forty-one nations in the TIMSS1995 science assessment.[3] Some of the countries have the same rank because of a convention: when there is a tie, those with the same score are assigned the average of the ranks involved. Thus, Bulgaria, the

---

3. The uses of *TIMSS* can be a little confusing. The *T* stood for "Third" in the original study conducted in 1995. However, studies were also conducted in 1999 and 2003 and the meaning of the *T* changed to "Trends." It is now customary to put the year of the administration after the letters, as in TIMSS1995 on this page.

Rank	Country	Percent Correct
1	SINGAPORE	70
2	Korea	66
3	Japan	65
4	Czech Republic	64
6	Bulgaria	62
6	Netherlands	62
6	Slovenia	62
9	England	61
9	Hungary	61
9	Austria	61
11.5	Belgium (Flemish)	60
11.5	Australia	60
14	Slovak Republic	59
14	Sweden	59
14	Canada	59
19	Ireland	58
19	UNITED STATES	58
19	Russian Federation	58
19	New Zealand	58
19	Norway	58
19	Hong Kong	58
19	Germany	58
23.5	Thailand	57
23.5	Israel	57
25.5	Switzerland	56
25.5	Spain	56
27	Scotland	55
28	France	54
29.5	Greece	52

FIG. 11   TIMSS Middle School Science Results (1996)

Rank	Country	Percent Correct
29.5	Iceland	52
31	Denmark	51
33.5	Latvia	50
33.5	Portugal	50
33.5	Belgium (French)	50
33.5	Romania	50
36	Lithuania	49
37.5	Iran	47
37.5	Cyprus	47
39	Kuwait	43
40	Colombia	39
41	SOUTH AFRICA	27
INTERNATIONAL AVERAGE = 56		

Source: *Science Achievement in the Middle School Years.* 1996.
Boston College, Chestnut Hill, Massachusetts.

Netherlands, and Slovenia all had a score of 62 and occupied ranks 5, 6, and 7. By the convention just mentioned, all three were assigned the rank of 6.

As noted, American kids were nineteenth, a rank just barely above average. But take a look at the scores to the right of the ranks. A different picture emerges. The nations bunch closely together. In fact, if American students had managed a mere 5 percent more correct, they would have shot all the way up the ladder to rank fifth in the world. Conversely, had they slipped a mere 5 percentage points, they would have fallen all the way to twenty-ninth. Imagine, 10 percentage points difference on a test equals twenty-four differences in rank.

Now there are times when tiny differences in scores have huge consequences, but this is not one of them. In recent Olympics, in some events the difference between a gold medal and a silver has been 0.01 second, one-one-hundredth of a second. I can't imagine that small differences on a multiple-choice test taken by thirteen-year-olds have any practical consequences for the students or for their nations.

> Principle of Data Interpretation: *Be aware of whether you are dealing with ranks or scores.*

Changes Over Time: Simpson's Paradox

It is quite common in analyses of educational trends for the whole group—which could be a school, a district, a state, or the nation—to show one trend or pattern and the subgroups to show the opposite. That sounds like a paradox, and it is. It is something that occurs so often in social sciences generally as well as in education that it has a name: Simpson's paradox.

> Simpson's paradox: *The aggregrate group shows one trend or pattern, but the subgroups show a different trend or pattern, usually the reverse trend.*

Concern for Simpson's paradox is built into No Child Left Behind (NCLB). NCLB requires that schools report test-score changes for different ethnic groups, low-income students, special education students, and so on. This requirement prevents the progress of one large group from obscuring the fact that possibly not all subgroups are showing growth.

First, let's consider the paradox in the abstract with a hypothetical set of data, which are given in Figure 12.

Let's say that the 500s in the column marked "Time 1" represent the SAT scores of white students while the 400s represents the SAT scores of minority students. If we add all the numbers up and divide by the number of numbers, we find that the mean SAT score at Time 1 is 480.

Now let's consider the numbers in the column marked "Time 2." This is a different group of students and Time 2 could be five, ten, or fifteen years after Time 1. It doesn't matter. At Time 2, we let the 510s represent the SAT scores of white students and the 430s represent the SAT scores of minority students.

Thus we see that SAT scores for whites have risen from 500 at Time 1 to 510 at Time 2. The SAT scores for minorities have risen from 400 at Time 1 to 430 at Time 2. Thus, all subgroups have rising SAT scores, and minority

	Time 1	Time 2
	500	510
	500	510
	500	510
	500	510
	500	510
	500	510
	500	430
	500	430
	400	430
	400	430
$\overline{X}$	480	478

FIG. 12   Hypothetical SAT Data

students have shown more growth than white students, thirty points versus ten points.

And, yet, when we calculate the mean at Time 2, it is only 478, lower than it was at Time 1. All subgroups gained, but the overall average has fallen. A paradox. Simpson's paradox. How can it be?

It can be because the *composition* of the group taking the SAT has changed from Time 1 to Time 2. At Time 1, minority students constituted 20 percent of the whole group while at Time 2, they constituted 40 percent. Their scores, while rising, are still lower than the scores of white students, but at Time 2 these improving-but-still-lower scores represent a larger proportion of the total number of scores.

Adding more and more students from lower-scoring groups can attenuate the overall increases and, in our hypothetical example, even cause the aggregate average to fall.

It has been argued that the lack of change in SAT scores represents stagnation of achievement, but, in fact, it only reflects demographic changes in the nation. These are shown in Figure 13.

In 1981, white students made up 85 percent of SAT test takers. In 2005, they accounted for only 63 percent. Other groups have seen increases.

If we look at the SAT verbal scores from 1981 and 2005, we see Simpson's paradox in action. For the nation as a whole, there is little change:

Ethnic Makeup of SAT Test-Taking Pool, 1981–2005		
	1981	2005
White	85	63
Black	9	12
Asian	3	11
Mexican	2	5
Puerto Rican	1	1
American Indian	0	1

FIG. 13   Changes in SAT Test Takers

four points in 24 years. The national average score is 504 in 1981 and 508 in 2005.[4] But when we look at the scores by ethnic subgroup, we see that every group's verbal average score has improved, in some cases by a large amount.

We should also note that the verbal average has risen despite an ever larger proportion of high school seniors taking the SAT each year (the mathematics average has also gone up). This would lead us to expect the average score to decline, as it represents a deeper and deeper dig into the talent pool. In 1981, 933,672 seniors, less than a third of the senior class, sat for the SAT. In 2002, 1,475,623 seniors, some 43 percent of the entire senior class, took the test.

We can see Simpson's paradox operating on a national scale by looking at SAT verbal scores from 1981 and 2005 (see Figure 14).

Simpson's paradox also affects the results of "the Nation's Report Card," the National Assessment of Educational Progress. Looking at the data by ethnicity reveals much larger gains than the aggregate results. (See Figure 15.)

> **Principle of Data Interpretation:** *Watch out for Simpson's paradox.*

4. This is not a genuine "national average" because only about 43 percent of the senior class takes the SAT and the percentage of seniors taking it in different states varies from 4 percent to 80 percent. The phrase is merely used for convenience.

Gains for Ethnic Groups—Verbal			
	1981	**2005**	**Gain**
Whites	519	529	10
Blacks	412	433	21
Asians	474	511	37
Mexicans	438	453	15
Puerto Ricans	437	460	23
American Indians	471	489	18
All Groups	504	508	4

FIG. 14   SAT Verbal Scores for 1981 and 2005

All Students	1978	2004	Gain
Age 9	219	241	22
Age 13	266	281	15
Age 17	300	307	7
Black	**1978**	**2004**	**Gain**
Age 9	190	224	34
Age 13	228	262	34
Age 17	270	285	15
Hispanic	**1978**	**2004**	**Gain**
Age 9	202	230	28
Age 13	239	265	26
Age 17	277	289	12
White	**1978**	**2004**	**Gain**
Age 9	225	247	22
Age 13	274	288	14
Age 17	310	313	3

For all three ages, minorities show greater gains than seen in the aggregate numbers.

Source: National Center for Education Statistics, U.S. Department of Education

FIG. 15   NAEP Math Scores Showing Simpson's Paradox

It is not only changes over time that bring Simpson's paradox into play. It appears whenever some subgroups differ on some major variable. What "some major variable" might be rests with the thoughtfulness and ingenuity of the researcher to realize what might be relevant. For instance, consider the table in Figure 16 on hospital mortality rates.

Hospitals are dangerous places; people who have one medical problem when they enter often develop other medical problems while there, especially pneumonia from drug-resistant bacteria. From the table, though, it looks like if you do have to check in, Hospital B is the medical facility of choice.

But what if we know some significant variable on which Hospital A differs from Hospital B? Suppose A specializes in difficult cases. Let's divide those one thousand patients into people who arrived at the hospital in good shape and people who arrived in bad shape. (See Figure 17.)

Well. You might want to call it a draw for people showing up in good shape, but A does have a 1 percent advantage. A lot more of the 1,000 people in our sample were suffering severely, though, when they arrived at Hospital A than at Hospital B, 210 versus 30. Yet a higher percentage of those, 53 percent, survived at A than at B, 30 percent. Arriving in good shape or bad, your chances of surviving are better at Hospital A.

	Survived	Died	Total	Survival Rate
Hospital A	800	200	1,000	80%
Hospital B	900	100	1,000	90%

FIG. 16   Hospital Mortality Rates for Two Hospitals

People Arriving in Good Shape	Survived	Died	Total	Survival Rate
Hospital A	590	10	600	98%
Hospital B	870	30	900	97%
People Arriving in Bad Shape	**Survived**	**Died**	**Total**	**Survival Rate**
Hospital A	210	190	400	53%
Hospital B	30	70	100	30%

FIG. 17   Mortality Rates for Two Hospitals by Condition on Arrival

3

Making Inferences, Finding Relationships

Statistical Significance and Correlation Coefficients

Statistical Significance

Few ideas in data analysis are more misunderstood than the concept of statistical significance. In part this misunderstanding is due to its technical nature. In part it is due to the inability of people to explain it simply. And in part it is due to its common use not as an instrument for understanding results but as a means of pushing a policy. Many a school board has been pressured into adopting something a superintendent wanted because he kept repeating that the study yielded "significant" results. The concept can, however, be explained in straightforward English.

A test for statistical significance can be applied to virtually any kind of statistical analysis, but here we will stick to the simplest case: Is the difference between two groups significant? Look at Figure 18.

Let's say that these two normal curves represent the results from tests given to two groups of young readers. One group learned to read with techniques that relied heavily on phonics. The other group learned with a more literature-based approach. When tested, there was a mean difference—call it D—between the two groups of five points. Did the one group score significantly higher than the other group?

To answer that question in this hypothetical example, we must make a number of assumptions. We must assume for the sake of argument that the test we gave was equally fair to both groups, a rather iffy assumption but

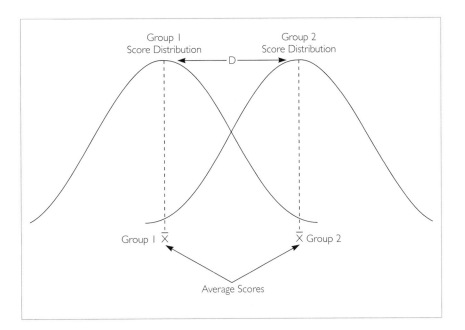

FIG. 18 Hypothetical Reading Test Results

one we need to make here. We must assume as well that the teachers of the two groups were equally skillful at teaching reading. We must also assume that the two groups did not differ in any way prior to the instruction that might have affected the results. If one group had higher previous scores or came from a more affluent neighborhood than the other, there might well be a difference between the two groups that has absolutely nothing to do with the quality of the reading programs. If groups do differ in ways that look important, there are statistical methods for adjusting for those differences, but I do not address those in this book.

We now run our statistical test. We don't, for the purposes here, need to know what that test is, but if you want to pursue it further, it's called a t-test for independent means.

Our statistical test allows us to answer this question: How likely were we to see a difference between the two groups as large as the one we did see, five points, if, in fact, there were really no differences between the two groups? Or, as statisticians like to say, how likely we were to see a difference as large as the one we did see if the two samples came from populations with the same mean?

To many people, these questions initially look meaningless. After all, we gave the tests, we saw a difference of five points, and that difference is real, right? Why do we need statistical tests in the first place? We need them because of two words I slipped into the last sentence of the preceding paragraph, *sample* and *population*. The difference of five points might not, in fact, be real.

Testing for statistical significance takes us back to the discussion of samples and populations on pages 46–47. If we didn't want to bother with statistical tests, we'd have to give a test to everyone. If we were testing at the fourth grade, that would mean giving it to more than 4 million students nationwide. Then, if we assumed our test was free of error, whatever difference we'd see would be real and we would need no statistical tests to tell us that. Statisticians would say that we had tested the whole population of fourth graders.

Nationally, though, we never test everyone, never test a population, although some states traditionally have tested all students in selected grades and the No Child Left Behind law now requires that all states do test everyone every year in grades 3–8 in reading and math. It is estimated that the law's testing requirements will cost the states $5.4 billion from 2002 to 2008. For most purposes, though, we have neither the money nor the manpower to test everyone, so we test a sample. But since it's a sample and not everybody, we might obtain a different result than if we tested everybody. Worse, we often have to use what statisticians call *samples of convenience*— usually the kids in the nearby schools. They might or might not be representative of the nation as a whole.

Because of the difficulty and cost, very few tests are given to nationally representative samples. The National Assessment of Educational Progress (NAEP) is one of the few testing programs that has the resources to try. It attempts to draw a representative sample of students, something that is also called a *national probability sample.* Currently, because the passage of NCLB made state-level NAEP mandatory, NAEP also draws a representative sample of each state (before NCLB, state-level NAEP was voluntary and each state paid for the testing and reporting).

But even drawing representative samples would not assure us that the two groups were identical. Drawing a representative sample removes any *systematic* bias, but one or more groups might be biased by chance. Just as an unbiased coin can come up heads six straight times by chance, so can a sample we hope is representative be biased by chance.

So, back to our reading experiment. We've done our statistical test. We will end up saying either that the difference is not significant or that it is significant at a particular level of probability. The choice of level is arbitrary, but there are conventions that govern the levels that researchers use. Most researchers will not report a result as significant unless it is significant at least at the .05 level.

What does "the .05 level" mean? Well, .05 can also be rendered as 5/100 or 1/20. The .05 level means the statistical test is telling us that seeing a difference as large as the one we did see, by chance alone, is less than five in one hundred or one in twenty. I prefer the .01 level of significance. If you're accepting the .05 level, you'll be wrong one time in twenty, and that seems to me too often if you're trying to build a science of educational research. At the .01 level, you'll be wrong only one time in a hundred; that is, once in a hundred times, you will pronounce a difference real when it isn't.

You will hear researchers say things like, "pea less than point oh five" or "pea less than point oh one." When written, "pea" is p, which is the symbol for probability, and "less than" is represented by the mathematical symbol $<$. Written, the two statements are $p < .05$ and $p < .01$. The statement $p < .05$ means that the probability is less than one in twenty that the difference as large as the one you saw could have occurred by chance, and the statement $p < .01$ means that the probability is less than one in one hundred that the difference as large as the one you saw could have occurred by chance.

What's critical for you to keep in mind always is that a statistically significant result might have no practical significance whatsoever.

> **Principle of Data Interpretation:** *Do not confuse statistical significance and practical significance.*

A statistically significant finding might have no practical ramifications because, in part, the chances of finding statistical significance vary with the size of the groups in the study—if we have very large groups, very small differences can be statistically significant.

This is easy to see by example. In fact, we've already seen a variation on it in our ears-of-corn experiment on pages 46–47. There we were trying to judge the quality of corn in only one field, and as we added more and more ears to our sample, we got more confident that our conclusion was correct. There we were concerned only about one field of corn. What we're doing with our significance tests is determining if the quality in two fields differs. As in the first example, if we picked only five ears in each, the difference would have to be really noticeable for us to conclude that the two fields differed. But as we added more and more ears to our samples, we would get more and more confident that any difference we saw was real. With a large sample, we would conclude that even a small difference was real.

Suppose in the reading instruction experiment mentioned earlier, we had a single classroom for each of the two groups, say 25 students. We would need a fairly sizable difference to conclude that a difference was significant (real). But what if we had 1 million students in each group? Given that there are about 4 million students in a grade, we're now running our experiment on about half of the population in that grade. We'd be much more confident that a small difference was real if we were testing half of the population (2 million students) than if we were testing only a tiny fraction of the population (50 students).

There is no magical or purely technical way to decide whether or not a statistically significant difference means you should do something different in your school. There are only tools that assist your judgment. There is no escape from using judgment.

One such tool that can assist judgment is called *effect size,* or ES. An ES is easy to calculate. You subtract the mean of the control group in an experiment from the mean of the experimental group and divide by the average of the standard deviations of the two groups. The formula is very simple:

$$ES = \frac{mean_E - mean_C}{\left(\dfrac{SD_E + SD_C}{2}\right)}$$

$mean_E$ = mean of experiment group
$mean_C$ = mean of control group

Now, I just performed a little linguistic sleight of hand mentioning the control group and the experimental group. In a pharmaceutical experiment we can readily identify these groups—the experimental group gets a new medication; the control group gets a sugar pill. The latter is called a placebo, and it's given to control for whether or not people will react to the situation independent of whether or not they've taken a drug. Some people will react to the *idea* of taking a medication as strongly as to the actual medication.

There is usually no equivalent to the placebo in educational research. A placebo is a nontreatment. In our reading experiment, we had no nontreatment. We had a phonics-based treatment and a literature-based treatment. If both of these treatments were new, then we probably would have included a third group and called it a control group, but it wouldn't have been a true control group—it would have been a group of students who were instructed in reading as they had been in years past. It would have really been a traditional group.

In any case, we subtract two means and divide by the average standard deviation to get an effect size. In our reading example, we had a five-point difference in the means, and let's say the mean of one group was 55 and the mean of the other was 50. Let's assume that the average standard deviation was also 5. Remember that with a mean of 50 and an SD of 5, 34 percent of all scores will be between 50 and 55, 34 percent between 45 and 50, 14 percent between 55 and 60, and 14 percent between 40 and 45—assuming a normal distribution. Our calculation becomes

$$\text{ES} = \frac{55 - 50}{5}, \text{ which becomes } \frac{5}{5}, \text{ which is } +1.0.$$

So the ES is +1.0. Education experiments almost never produce effect sizes this large, and I'm using it only because it makes the interpretation easier to explain.

What we've got here is called a *standard score,* but it's a standard score for groups as opposed to the more commonly seen standard score for individuals. Standard scores are discussed in detail on pages 159–162, and you might want to skip to that discussion before continuing here.

If we find an ES of +1.0 it means that our research treatment is the equivalent of having moved the students a full standard deviation. If we assume that the control group was at the fiftieth percentile (an assumption of convenience), then our experimental group would have been at the eighty-fourth percentile (ahead of the 34 percent of people who score between the mean and +1 standard deviations and the 50 percent of people who score below the mean).

An effect size doesn't remove the need for people to make judgments. How large an effect size do we need before thinking it has practical implications? Researchers differ on this, but generally, effect sizes between +0.20 and +0.30 are where most people think an ES has practical ramifications. For example, if we could find an instructional treatment that produced an effect size of +0.30 in achievement for African Americans three years in a row versus some more traditional instructional treatment, we would come very close to wiping out the black-white achievement gap.

And, an ES is not all you need to consider. For instance, suppose in an experiment one curriculum is found to produce larger gains in achievement than another and that the resulting effect size is +.22. Do you recommend to the board to adopt the curriculum? What if it costs five times as much or requires many hours of professional training for teachers and is still hard to work with? Some kind of formal or informal cost-benefit analysis needs to play a role, too.

Correlation and Its Discontents

In some despairing moments, I am tempted to found the National Association for the Abolition of Correlation Coefficients. Although the correlation coefficient can be a useful statistic, it causes a great deal of mischief. It creates havoc because people so often misinterpret it. I think that we tend to misinterpret the correlation coefficient because our brains are hardwired to do so. Our brains see correlations in the natural world and make causal inferences about them. Overall, no doubt, these inferences yield useful results. As a species we probably wouldn't have survived if our brains didn't make them. Causal inferences from correlations have good survival value.

But a correlation coefficient is a specific statistic from which, for a single study, *no causal inference is permitted.* The correlation coefficient plots how one variable varies as another variable also varies. If children's test scores correlate positively with parents' educational level, as the educational level goes up, the test scores go up. The size of the correlation coefficient tells us how strong the relationship is.

> **Principle of Data Interpretation:** *Make no causal inferences from correlation coefficients.*

If children's test scores correlate negatively with poverty, as poverty increases, test scores go down. And once again, the size of the correlation tells us how strong the relationship is.

To get from correlation to causation, one needs substantial additional evidence and experiments to rule out other possible causes than the cause you suspect. For instance, for many years the tobacco industry argued that the research linking smoking to cancer was only correlational. There might be a few that would argue it still despite twenty-eight reports from the surgeon general's office that provide a multitude of evidence, but most people believe there is a causal relationship. In addition to seeing a correlation between smoking and cancer, there is evidence about the increased life spans and decreased cancer incidence from people who have ceased smoking.

Correlation questions abound in research about schools: Is there a correlation between absenteeism and later dropping out? Is there a correlation between teacher experience and student achievement? Is there a correlation between courses taken in high school and success in college? Is there a correlation between class size and achievement? Is there a correlation between per-pupil expenditures and achievement? And so on.

Correlation coefficients can take on values between −1.0 and +1.0. A correlation of −1.0 means there is a perfect relationship between two variables: as one gets larger (say, percent of students in poverty), the other gets smaller (those students' test scores) in a perfectly predictable way. A correlation of +1.0 also describes a perfect correlation, but as one variable increases, so does the other one in a perfectly predictable way. The key phrase in the past two sentences is *perfectly predictable.* For correlations smaller than −1.0 or +1.0, as one variable changes, the other variable changes, but not in a perfectly predictable way. A correlation of 0.0 denotes a zero correlation: from the value of one variable, you can't tell anything about the value of the other variable. If there were a zero correlation between SAT scores and college success, then people who scored a perfect 800 would flunk out as frequently as people who scored 200, the lowest possible score.

> **Principle of Data Interpretation:** *Any two variables can be correlated. The resultant correlation coefficient might or might not be meaningful.*

We can correlate any two variables. Whether or not the resulting correlations make sense is another question. Before everyone started wearing jeans, the Dow Jones stock market index correlated with skirt length. Shorter skirts were associated with economic good times and a rising market. Longer skirts were correlated with recessions. To the best of my knowledge, no one suggested raising hemlines as a means to boost the stock market. Similarly, there is a correlation between arm length and shirtsleeve length. Given *only* a correlation coefficient, though, it makes as much sense to think that increasing sleeve length will make arms grow longer as it does to think that longer arms will mean longer sleeves. In this case other information could be adduced to assist in determining which way the causal relationship would operate.

The correlation coefficient answers the question As one variable changes, how does a second variable change? It measures the relationship, nothing more or less. Let me illustrate this with a hypothetical experiment: We find six pairs of parents who have identical IQs and who also have just given birth to identical twins. We convince these parents to let cognitive and developmental psychologists raise one of each pair of twins, applying their expertise to increase the children's cognitive skills. The parents raise the other child, whom we'll call Twin 1. Consider these hypothetical results:

Parents' IQ	Twin 1 IQ	Twin 2 IQ
100	100	130
101	101	131
102	102	132
103	103	133
104	104	134
105	105	135

Now we ask the question: What is the correlation between parents' IQ and the IQ of Twin 1? It's fairly easy to see that since the child's IQ is identical to that of the parents, the correlation is +1.0. As the parents' IQ rises, the child's IQ rises in a perfectly predictable way.

What is the correlation between parents' IQ and the IQ of Twin 2? It is also +1.0. The correlation measures the relationship of two variables, and as the parents' IQ rises, Twin 2's IQ rises in a perfectly predictable way.

Obviously, though, whatever those cognitive scientists did had some impact on those Twin 2s. They each have IQs that are thirty points higher than their corresponding Twin 1. For most IQ tests, the standard deviation is fifteen points, so our little experiment raised the IQs of Twin 2 by two standard deviations. The mean on IQ tests is set to 100. Recall that there are always 34 percent of scores between the mean and +1 SD and that there are always 14 percent of scores between +1 SD and +2 SD; that means that we have moved the Twin 2s to the ninety-eighth percentile (34 + 14 + the 50 percent of the scores that are below the mean). That's quite an outcome.

This experiment carries importance in spite of the fact that no one ever did it. It illustrates that how people interpret the outcome of an experiment depends in part on what kind of statistic the research used. For over a century a debate has raged as to whether nature (genes) or nurture (environment) is more important in determining children's IQs. In this case, looking at the *correlation* between parents' IQs and children's IQs makes it seem like genes play an enormous role in determining IQ. But if we look at the *difference* between parents' IQs and children's IQs for that second twin, it looks like the environment plays a large role as well.

The twins experiment casts light on one reason that different researchers emphasize nature or nurture. Workers conducting correlational analyses often see large correlations between measures on parents and children or among siblings and conclude that genes play a large role in psychological characteristics. Researchers looking for *differences* between different groups treated in different ways (as with the twins raised by parents versus those raised by cognitive psychologists) often find such differences and conclude that the environment has a powerful influence.

To repeat an earlier statement, any two variables can be correlated, but only some correlations are meaningful and useful. When admissions officers at universities use the SAT to predict college freshmen's grade point averages, they calculate the correlation coefficient between the scores on the SAT and the grades students earn in their freshman year. If a college has more applicants than spaces, the SAT can be used as one factor (and only one factor among many) in choosing the students who are most likely to be successful in that college.

Along with the tendency to make causal inferences from correlation coefficients, there is also a tendency, not quite as strong, to think of any observed correlation as being perfect. In the case of the correlation between the SAT and freshman grades, the correlation is only .45. This means that some students with high SAT scores will do well in college and some will not. And some students with relatively low SAT scores will do well in college and some will not.

> **Principle of Data Interpretation:** *Make no causal inferences from correlation coefficients.*

Yet many people tend to think of the SAT–grade point correlation as perfect. Indeed, Nicholas Lemann's 1999 book, *The Big Test: The Secret History of the SAT,* presented the test as *the* life-determining event in a high school student's academic career. When I conducted background research in preparation for a review of *The Big Test,* I found that some highly selective colleges seemed to give more weight to the SAT than others. Stanford leaned heavily on the test in admissions decisions. On the other hand, Brown University, which could fill *two* freshman classes just with applicants with SAT verbal scores between 750 and 800 (750 being slightly above the ninety-ninth percentile and 800 being a perfect score), appeared to give more weight to other factors. For instance, it admitted only one-third of those who scored between 750 and 800.

And that tendency to make causal inferences from correlations remains strong. A few years back, the College Board reported that students who took algebra early (eighth or ninth grade) went on to take a rigorous high school curriculum and were likely to attend four-year colleges. The board labeled algebra a "gateway" course and recommended that schools offer it to more students so that they, too, would take a tough academic regimen in high school and go on to a four-year college. More recently, algebra II has been identified as *the* gateway course (Carnevale and Desrochers 2004, viii).

I don't have actual data to refute the College Board, but its conclusion represents a causal interpretation of a correlation coefficient. I think it might well be wrong. I would interpret the correlation differently: Schools, whether we like it or not, sort students. They identify talent. Teachers, counselors, and administrators identify the students they think can handle an algebra class or an IB program or whatever. The identification process is certainly not perfect, but I think this is likely what's going on: Kids whom the schools funnel into algebra early are those who the school thinks will go on to take solid and trig and maybe calculus, plus natural sciences, and then head to a four-year institution of higher education. Early taking of algebra doesn't lead to a four-year institution; it reflects the selection process extant in schools.

A few paragraphs ago, I put the typical SAT–grade point correlation at .45. What does a correlation of .45 mean? It means that there is a relationship between SAT scores and success in college, but the relationship is not perfect. There are two commonly used correlation coefficients, officially known as the Pearson product-moment correlation coefficient and the Pearson rank-order coefficient. If the statistic is referred to just as "the correlation coefficient," then you can assume it is the product-moment version, and this is the one most often calculated. Both can vary between -1.0 and $+1.0$. The product-moment coefficient is represented in texts by the letter r, and the rank-order coefficient by the Greek letter *rho* (ρ). The rank-order coefficient is an approximation of the product-moment correlation. The product-moment correlation is used anytime we have continuous variables like test scores.

We earlier spoke of performing statistical tests to determine if the difference between two groups was statistically significant. We can perform significance tests on correlations too. In this instance, though, we are not looking at whether or not a difference is significant but whether the correlation coefficient is sufficiently large to say that it is significantly different from zero.

A graph of the variables in a correlation helps provide an intuitive, gut-level feel for what the relationship looks like. One variable in the correlation is placed on the horizontal axis and other on the vertical axis of the graph. The four graphs—they are called *scatter plots*—in Figure 19 show an almost perfect positive correlation, a perfect negative correlation, an almost zero correlation, and the correlation of +.45, the average correlation between SAT scores and freshman college grade points. I've labeled the axes for this graph, with the horizontal axis being the SAT score, which can go from 200 to 800, and the vertical axis being the college freshman grade point average, which can go from 0 to 4.0. As you can see, knowing the SAT allows you to predict the grade point average the students will attain as college freshmen, but that prediction is far from perfect.

Look at the correlation between SAT and GPA. Visually, it forms an oval. Now look at the perfect negative correlation in scatter plot 2. It's a straight line. As a correlation increases in size from 0.0 to +1.0 or −1.0, the scatter plot becomes an ever thinner oval until at +1.0 or −1.0 it collapses into a straight line.

The product-moment coefficient is used to calculate the relationship between continuous variables, variables that can take on any value within a given range. SAT scores are continuous with values from 200 to 800. Annual salary is a continuous variable. So is a grade point average, although the range is relatively narrow.

In contrast to continuous variables are ranks. The World Economic Forum each year publishes the *Global Competitiveness Report,* which combines many variables to rank 117 countries from 1 to 117 on their global competitiveness. If you had ranks for these countries on a test taken by students in all 117 nations, you could calculate the rank-order correlation coefficient between the test-score ranks and the competitiveness ranks. FYI: In spite of generally average ranks in international comparisons of test scores, the United States ranks number 1 in global competitiveness.

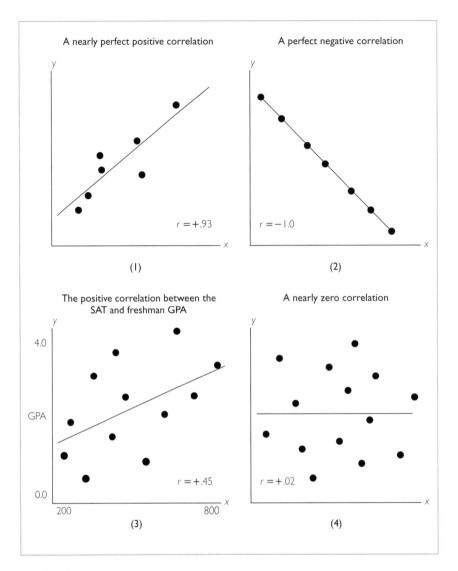

FIG. 19 Scatter Plots

In fact, both the continuous variable and the rank correlation coefficients *assume* that the relationship between the two variables, no matter how large or small, is linear. This means there is another good reason to look at a scatter plot of the correlation: to get a look at whether the relationship really is linear or not. Figure 20 indicates that there is a strong correlation between the two variables, but it won't show up in a correlation coefficient because the relationship between the two variables is curvilinear, not linear. A scatter

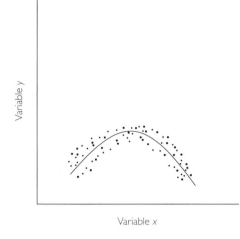

Variable *x*

FIG. 20 Scatter Plot Showing Curvilinear
Correlation Between Variables *x* and *y*

plot is not absolutely essential to seeing a curvilinear relationship—there are statistical tests to determine if such a relationship exists—but the scatter plot is perhaps the easiest way to see the actual relationship.

Comparing the Incomparable

We need to alert ourselves to a common problem in interpreting correlations: using groups that are not comparable. We have already talked about ensuring that groups are comparable over time (pages 58–59). But we must also make certain that in any correlation, the groups being used are comparable.

The most notorious stories about noncomparable groups involve the SAT. Before 1983, the College Board released state-level SAT data only to each state. At the time I headed the testing programs in Virginia, and each year a board staff member would fly up from the board's Atlanta office and meet with the state superintendent, associate superintendents, and me. He spoke in hushed tones as if he were delivering highly classified, your-eyes-only information.

One year, 1982, I think, an enterprising journalist in Ohio called all fifty states, obtained their SAT averages, and ranked the states. This caused brows to furrow. Everyone expected to see Connecticut and Massachusetts with high ranks. These are traditionally high-scoring states. But Mississippi, a typically low-scoring state on tests, outdid them. The media were baffled, as were some educators.

The reason for the strange rankings was quite straightforward: states do not require everyone to take the SAT and in some states it is not the preferred admissions test. In 1982, northeastern states and southern states along the Atlantic seaboard favored it. Somewhere between 50 percent and 70 percent of the seniors in those states took the SAT. In Mississippi, only 3 percent did. Mississippi, and a number of Deep South, Midwestern, and high plains states favored the ACT, the college admissions battery produced by the American College Testing Program in Iowa City. In those states, students who took the SAT were students attempting to attend East Coast or West Coast colleges that required the SAT as part of an admissions application.

A study published in the *Harvard Educational Review* shortly after the uproar showed that most of the variance in state-level SAT scores was accounted for by variations in the proportion of students who took the test (Powell and Steelman 1996). This makes intuitive sense—if nearly 75 percent of the seniors in one state are compared with an elite 3 percent in another state, they're not going to look very good.

Still, former secretary of education William Bennett looked at state-level SAT averages and state-level spending on education and pronounced the correlation between money and achievement to be zero, at least achievement as measured by the SAT (many would argue that the SAT is not a test of achievement). Bennett did not actually calculate a correlation coefficient, but merely pointed to some high-scoring states that didn't spend a lot of money and to some lower-scoring states that did.

Washington Post pundit George Will pounced on this data with a 1993a column titled "Meaningless Money Factor" (conservative journalists, economists, and politicians seem to spend much of their time trying to find evidence that money is not correlated with educational achievement). Will observed that New Jersey spent more money on K–12 education than any other state in the union but finished only thirty-ninth in the great SAT race. Once again, though, the important factor was the percent of students taking the test. In the year of Will's column, 76 percent of the seniors in New Jersey had taken the test while only 4 percent in states like Utah, Mississippi, and Alabama had. One could congratulate New Jersey for motivating more than three-quarters of its seniors to apply to four-year institutions that require the SAT, but Bennett and Will chose to complain about New Jersey's allegedly inefficient spending habits.

Before leaving correlation, we must consider one other factor that influences the size of the correlation coefficient: restriction of range. Again, we have in restriction of range a technical construct that is readily explained in everyday language. Suppose you wish to investigate the correlation between height and ability to play basketball. But suppose that everyone who volunteers for your study stands six feet six inches tall. Your correlation will always come up zero because the variable you're interested in, height, has no range. This is the limiting case of restriction of range: there isn't any range at all. If you were to find some people who were six feet five inches and six feet seven inches, you might find a correlation, but your range would still be quite narrow. If you could extend your range from five feet four inches to seven feet eight inches, you might well find a correlation (but you might not: it's an empirical question). At least under these circumstances your range of heights would be substantial.

I noted earlier that Stanford seemed to rely more on the SAT than some other selective schools. When I was a teaching assistant there in the 1960s, 22 percent of incoming freshmen had never seen a single B in their high school career. The 1960s was before people started worrying about grade inflation. Given the restricted range of grade points, the high school GPA did not predict college grades well. The average total SAT score was about 1250, quite high, but still at a point that produced some range, from about 950 to 1600. A range like this allows differential predictions.

One other correlation coefficient you might run into is called the *point biserial* (who names these things?). When constructing a test, the developer wants to keep "good" items and discard "bad" items. If judged OK on content, good and bad test items are then defined in terms of their statistical properties. One way of asking if an item is good or bad is to correlate the chances that a person will get the item right with the person's total test score. If an item is good, those who score high on the test overall will tend to get it right. If the developer finds an item that high scorers get wrong more often than low scorers, or an item that low scorers get right more often than high scorers, the developer will likely conclude that there is something peculiar about the item and discard it.

The point biserial alone doesn't determine whether a test item is good or bad. Items must be reviewed as well for ethnic, cultural, and gender biases.

We end this section with a variation on our opening theme: finding correlations is one instance of what we human beings do well: see patterns. In the May 2005 *Scientific American,* writer Michael Shermer put it this way:

Human beings evolved brains that are pattern-recognition machines, adept at detecting signals that enhance or threaten survival amid a very noisy world. This capability is association learning—associating the causal connections between A and B—as when our ancestors associated the seasons with the migration of game animals. We are skilled enough at it to have survived and passed on the genes for the capacity of association learning.

Unfortunately, the system has flaws. Superstitions are false associations—A appears to be connected to B, but it is not—the baseball player who doesn't shave and hits a home run. Or Aunt Mildred's cancer that went into remission after she imbibed extract of seaweed. (37)

The last example, Shermer notes, at least offers the *possibility* of a causal interpretation if we do the experiment right. All we need is a pool of cancer patients where we randomly assign half of them to a group that takes extract of seaweed and the other half to a group that takes a placebo.

If you're wondering about the ethics of giving sugar pills to people with cancer, keep in mind that at the start of the experiment we don't know if seaweed helps. Before we launch the experiment, we should certainly have some reason better than just Aunt Mildred's remission to think it might help. If treatments in experiments such as this look unusually effective early on, the researchers terminate the experiment, offer the treatment to the control group, and make the results public.

The Fine Art of Graphs

A picture might be worth a thousand words, but it might take many more than a thousand words to correct a misleading graph. Advances in software have helped educators create better graphs, but they still don't pay enough attention to the fine art of graphing. It is an art form, and if a graph is done badly it can badly mislead.

Consider Figure 21. Many consider this graph, which probably looks like a squiggly mess at first, to be the finest graph ever constructed, the creation of one Charles Joseph Minard. Minard depicted the consequences to the French army of Napoleon's Russian campaign. The starting point of interest is the great gray swath on the left side of the graph. The width of the swath represents the number of men in Napoleon's army as he entered Russia from Poland in 1812. Minard used one millimeter (about one-sixteenth of an

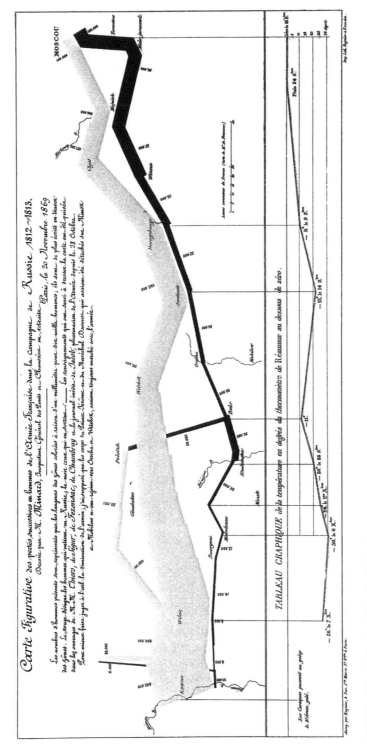

FIG. 21 Minard's Graph of Napoleon's March

inch) to represent each 10,000 men, and the army launched the Russian campaign with 422,000 troops. The swath immediately starts to dwindle, and by the time Napoleon reaches Moscow, only 100,000 troops remain.

The swath now changes color and reverses direction, reflecting Napoleon's retreat from Moscow. The swath continues to shrink. At the bottom of the graph, Minard plotted the temperature showing the depth of the Russian winter during Napoleon's retreat (the scale is the Réaumur, similar to Celsius in that water freezes at zero). The army suffered temperatures that never rose above zero after early November and which sank to a low of thirty below on December 6. By the time the graph returns to its starting point in Poland, a mere 10,000 men remain. The juxtaposition of the 422,000 men against the 10,000 at the same point on the paper is stunning.

Or consider Figure 22, another classic graph, developed during an 1854 cholera epidemic in a London neighborhood. At the time, people still considered foul vapors and divine retribution possible causes of disease. (Pat Robertson still does.) Physician John Snow plotted the deaths due to cholera according to where people lived. On the graph, each dot represents a death. The Xs represent the location of the area's eleven water pumps. Snow noticed that there was a strong correlation between where people lived and whether or not someone died: most deaths occurred near the Broad Street pump.

But that was just a correlation, and it wasn't perfect: some deaths occurred away from Broad Street's pump. Why did they die? Snow visited families who had suffered a death but who lived closer to another of the pumps than to the one on Broad Street. Some had children who attended a school near the Broad Street pump and others used that pump because they thought the water there tasted better.

Snow now knew that (1) most of the people afflicted lived near the Broad Street pump, and (2) people who were afflicted and who didn't live near the Broad Street pump had some other connection that led them to it.

With this knowledge, Snow now made a causal bet: something in the water at the Broad Street pump was causing the disease. Snow showed his findings to the neighborhood's vestrymen and asked permission to remove the handle, rendering the pump useless. The vestrymen agreed to remove the handle, and in a few days the epidemic that had killed more than five hundred had ended.

In his 2000 book, *Visual Revelations,* National Board of Medical Examiners statistician Howard Wainer observes that the Broad Street pump has been replaced by the John Snow Pub.

Yards

| 50 | 0 | 50 | 100 | 150 | 200 |

x Pump   • Deaths from cholera

FIG. 22   1854 Cholera Epidemic

One of the most remarkable inferences from a graph was made by Abraham Wald during World War II. Wald was assigned to determine where to put extra armor on planes, the better to protect them. He studied the patterns of bullet holes on planes returning from missions. This is shown schematically in Figure 23.

The white plane has no bullet holes. The darker plane has bullet holes everyplace except in the areas marked with white ovals. Wald's conclusion: put the extra armor where the white ovals are. But why would you add armor to planes where they *haven't* been shot?

Wald reasoned this way: In all likelihood, the planes got shot uniformly in every area, including the white ovals. Those shot in the darkened areas managed to return. Otherwise, Wald could not have studied them. Those that had been shot in the white oval areas must have failed to make it back

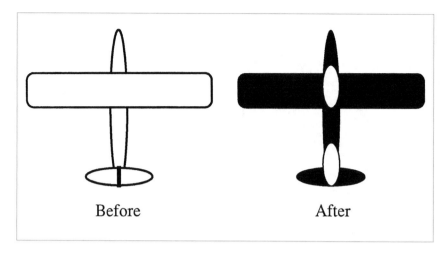

FIG. 23 Plane Armor (adapted from Wainer 2000)

to base. So, they should put the extra armor on these places of heightened vulnerability.

Notice that the impact of the graphs is from what they show, not necessarily how they show it. Wainer makes this general statement about good and bad graphs: "When looking at a good graph, your reaction should never be 'What a great graph!,' but 'What interesting data!' A good graph never calls too much attention to itself" (2000, 11).

There are many ways to construct a graph badly. Perhaps the most common error in education could be called the Case of the Missing Scale. It is shown in Figure 24a. Pictorially, it appears that school 1 showed a whopping test-score gain compared with school 2. Pictorially. When one actually looks at the change in percentile ranks on the vertical scale on the left, one can calculate that school 1 did gain twice as many percentile ranks as school 2, but neither gain is particularly large: two percentile ranks in the one case, four in the other.

The gain for school 1 *looks* big because the graph begins at the fiftieth percentile; half the scale is missing. Figure 24b shows that same data with the entire scale. The changes now look appropriately modest.

"Chop off the bottom." That was the advice Darrel Huff gave graphers in *How to Lie with Statistics* (1954). "Of course the eye doesn't 'understand' what isn't there, and a small rise has become, visually, a big one" (62).

Sometimes, space limits will prevent you from showing the whole scale. In such cases, the scale begins at zero, but some marks are inserted to show that part of the scale is missing, as in Figure 24c.

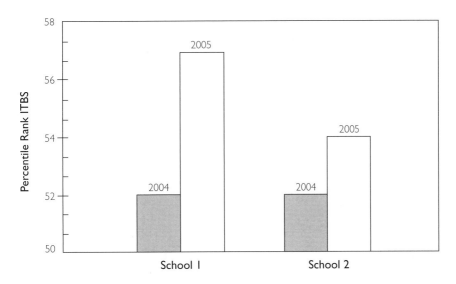

FIG. 24a Case of the Missing Scale

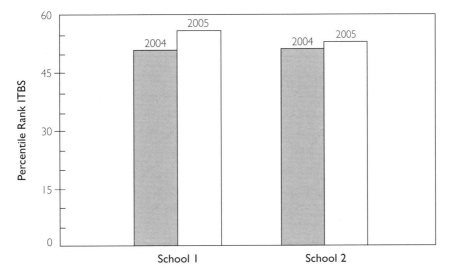

FIG. 24b Graph Showing Appropriate Scale

Sometimes graphs are poorly drawn out of naïveté. Sometimes they are deliberately distorted to help make a point, a point that might or might not be resident in the data themselves. Consider Figure 25a, from a 1992 article by Charles Murray and Richard Herrnstein, "What's Really Behind the SAT-Score Decline?" Because Murray and Herrnstein wanted people to believe that there really was an SAT decline and that it was large and important,

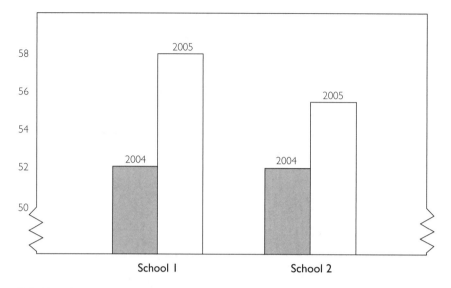

FIG. 24c   Graph Showing Part of Scale Is Missing

they might have chosen to draw Figure 25a as they did to help lead readers to that conclusion. As you can see, this is another instance of the Case of the Missing Scale. In this case, not only is the bottom chopped off, as Huff advised, but the top is as well. SAT scores range from 200 to 800. But the Murray–Herrnstein graph shows only a range from 400 to 500. Put on a six hundred-point scale, the declines would seem much smaller. The distortion was compounded somewhat because the periodical that carried the article, the recently defunct *Public Interest,* was a physically small journal.

Now consider Figure 25b. This graph appeared in a report titled *Perspectives on Education in America,* first created in late 1990, but not published until 1993 because the document, better known simply as the Sandia report, was suppressed by the first Bush administration[1] (Carson et al 2003). The Sandia report was printed on ordinary-sized 8½-by-11-inch paper. This alone would have spread the data out somewhat more than in *The Public Interest.* But the Sandia engineers who compiled the report wanted to show

---

1. The official story from then assistant secretary of education Diane Ravitch was that the report was undergoing "peer review" and was not yet ready for publication. That a report produced by one agency, the Department of Energy, would be reviewed by other agencies, the Department of Education and the National Science Foundation, was unprecedented. After the vice president of Sandia National Laboratories, who had overseen the compilation of the report, retired, I called him and asked if it really had been suppressed. He said, "Yes, it was definitely suppressed." The report appeared as the entirety of the May/June 1993 issue of the *Journal of Educational Research.*

READING EDUCATIONAL RESEARCH

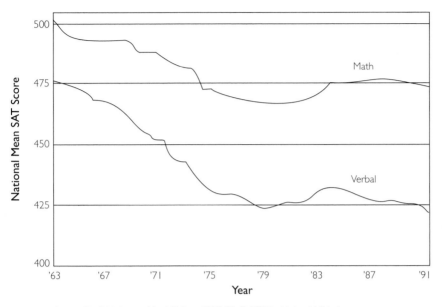

Source: *The Public Interest*, No. 6 (Winter 1992): 33. © 1999 by National Affairs, Inc.

FIG. 25a   Decline in SAT Scores, Graphed on a One-Hundred-Point Axis

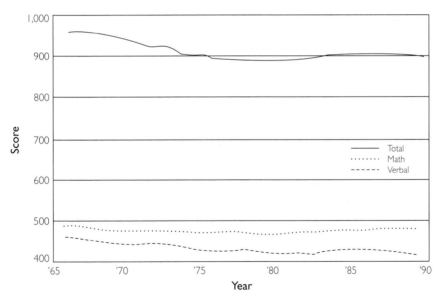

Source: C. C. Carson, R. M. Huelskamp, and T. D. Woodall. 1992. "Perspectives on Education in America."
Journal of Educational Research 86: 259–310.

FIG. 25b   Decline in SAT Scores, Graphed on a Six-Hundred-Point Axis

the change in the verbal and mathematics score combined as well as separately.

The Sandia engineers didn't use the full scale either. That would have gone from 400 to 1600. But the engineers did use a scale six times as large as the Murray-Herrnstein scale, ranging from 400 to 1000.

Look at the Murray–Herrnstein graph and then at the bottom two lines of the Sandia graph. The Murray–Herrnstein graph might lead people to use words like *plunge* or *plummet* to describe the fall of SAT scores. The Sandia graph is much less dramatic. *But they show the same data!* Only the scales are different.

The scales that one uses in graphing can convey very different pictorial impressions. You must learn to "see through" graphs.

> **Principle of Data Interpretation:** *Learn to "see through"*
> *graphs to determine what information they actually contain.*

Scales can be manipulated to alter the appearance and the impression a graph makes. Figure 26a was initially on the homepage of the U.S. Department of Education. Despite receiving widespread criticism, it remained part of *No Child Left Behind: A Toolkit for Teachers.* This graph is so deceptive that Wainer and a Harvard colleague, Daniel Koretz, devoted an entire article to it in the journal *Chance,* a publication of the American Statistical Association (Wainer and Koretz 2003).

How does this graph deceive? Let me count the ways. First, though, let's describe its components. Going from left to right, we see a set of bars representing how much money the federal government has spent on education each year under the Elementary and Secondary Education Act (ESEA). This was the 1965 act that brought Title I into existence and it has received periodic reauthorization. Since the 2001 reauthorization it has been commonly known as the No Child Left Behind Act.

Also going from left to right is a thick line beginning in 1975 for a NAEP fourth-grade reading score.

The left vertical scale shows the total number of federal dollars appropriated for education spending. On the right a second, independent vertical scale displays NAEP reading scores with a single point identified as 500.

The obvious intent of the graph is to convince the reader that although federal spending on education has greatly increased over time, reading

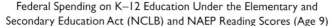

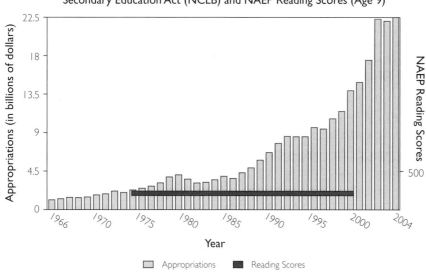

Federal Spending on K–12 Education Under the Elementary and Secondary Education Act (NCLB) and NAEP Reading Scores (Age 9)

Note: Appropriations for NCLB do not include funding for special education.
Source: U.S. Department of Education Budget Service and NAEP *1999 Trends in Academic Progress*

FIG. 26a   Federal Spending and NAEP Reading Trends

scores have been flat. Either schools have not spent the money wisely or, as is often said, throwing money at the problem doesn't work.

Some problems with this graph: First, why would one try to show this using *federal* expenditures? Even with the increases under NCLB, federal monies account for only about 7 to 8 percent of school budgets. Second, the line for reading scores stops in 1999. But the greatest increases in federal spending occurred in 2000 through 2004. The greatest spending increases occurred in years when there are no test data. So we don't know what's happened to reading scores in those years. Third, why would anyone expect there to be a direct link between federal spending and NAEP?

Fourth, the graph shows *total* spending. But since 1985, K–12 enrollments have soared. *Total* spending would have increased even if the per-pupil expenditures remained the same. Per-pupil spending is the appropriate scale for that left vertical axis. When Wainer and Koretz converted to per-pupil spending, they found that as spending rose, *mirabile dictu*, scores rose.

This graph also takes us back to earlier principles of data interpretation: watch for selectivity in the data and beware of Simpson's paradox. Where are the graphs for mathematics and science? For other ages? Where are the graphs by ethnicity—we saw earlier that NAEP scores reported by ethnicity show more growth than NAEP scores reported in the aggregate.

That 500 on the right-hand side of the graph is the upper limit for NAEP reading scores *for all three ages combined.* NAEP tests ages nine, thirteen, and seventeen. To show the combined scale for only one age, age nine, is wrong. Moreover, NAEP scores grow some ten to twelve points per year. Eighth graders typically score forty to fifty points higher than fourth graders. To put ten points a year of growth on a five-hundred-point scale, even if it were the appropriate scale, is to guarantee you won't see much growth. As Wainer and Koretz put it, using the five-hundred-point scale "preordains the appearance of stasis even when moderately sizable changes are taking place" (2003, 45). That single point, 500, is the only number on the right side of the graph, but the label "NAEP reading scores" gives the impression that the scale for reading scores runs all the way to the top when, in fact, the 500 is the scale's upper limit.

Finally, there is no connection between the left vertical axis, spending, and the right vertical axis, NAEP reading scores. This is not necessarily a misleading aspect of a graph, but it gives the grapher lots of room to manipulate the impression the graph makes. Wainer and Koretz again: "[This] allows the plotter (in the pejorative sense) to play any game at all, making the variables shown appear to have whatever relationship is desired" (46). "In the pejorative sense" are Wainer and Koretz's words, not an insertion by this author. By playing games and changing the scales, Wainer and Koretz show that the graph can give the impression that scores rose when funding stayed the same or even that scores rose as spending declined.

In May 2004, the Department of Education revised the toolkit for teachers and morphed the graph into the one shown in Figure 26b. Is the new graph any better? Well, the legend does specify that the unit is in constant 2004 dollars, something omitted from the original. The NAEP scores on the right vertical axis are more appropriate, but still arbitrary. The left vertical axis, though, still shows total dollars, not the more appropriate per-pupil amount.

Almost twenty years of funding and a decade of test scores have been lopped off. The graph now begins in 1984, not 1966. Could it be that those years were axed because there were *not* large increases in federal spending?

If anything, the new graph is more misleading than the original because another year of spending has been added, but the test data still end in 1999. In July 2005, though, the U.S. Department of Education released NAEP trend data that included the 2004 assessment—and scores had risen.

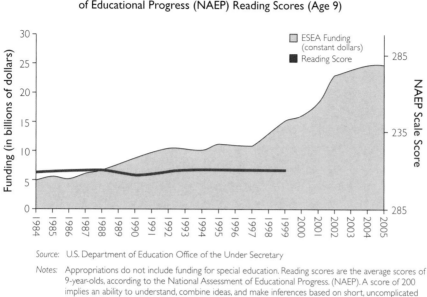

Federal Spending on K–12 Education Under the Elementary and Secondary Education Act (ESEA) and National Assessment of Educational Progress (NAEP) Reading Scores (Age 9)

Source: U.S. Department of Education Office of the Under Secretary

Notes: Appropriations do not include funding for special education. Reading scores are the average scores of 9-year-olds, according to the National Assessment of Educational Progress. (NAEP). A score of 200 implies an ability to understand, combine ideas, and make inferences based on short, uncomplicated passages about specific or sequentially related information.

FIG. 26b   New Version of NAEP Reading Trends Graph

Double-axis deceptions are especially easy to find (Wainer, in *Visual Revelations*, devotes a whole chapter to them), but single-axis graphs can also be manipulated by squeezing or expanding a scale to alter the impression. Huff's examples do nicely. He begins with the graph in Figure 27a, which shows in a proper graph (notice the scale starts at 0) that national income rose 10 percent in a year. Huff comments:

> Your ten percent *looks* like ten percent—an upward trend that is substantial but perhaps not overwhelming. That is very well if all you want to do is convey information. But suppose you wish to win an argument, shock a reader, move him to action or sell him something. For that, this chart lacks schmaltz. Chop off the bottom. (62)

I'm not sure that Huff was clear on either the literal meaning of *schmaltz* (rendered goose or chicken fat) or the colloquial meaning (sentimental, mawkish), but we'll let that go. He probably meant something like pizzazz. Cutting off the bottom gives us Figure 27b.

But why stop there? "Simply change the proportion between the ordinate and the abscissa," says Huff. "There's no rule against it, and it does give

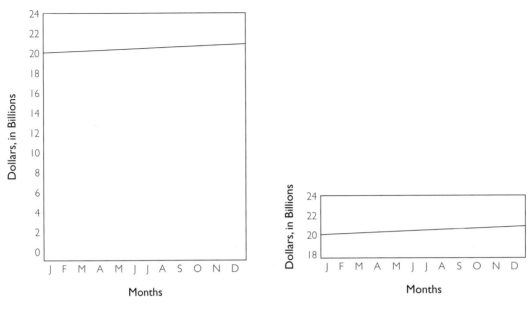

FIG. 27a Appropriate Graph

FIG. 27b Chopped-Off Graph

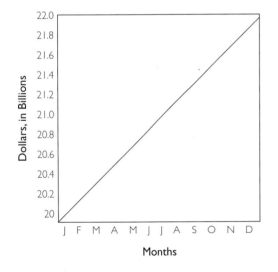

FIG. 27c Distorted Scale Graph

your graph a prettier shape" (63). Huff then lets each mark on the ordinate (the vertical axis) represent only one tenth as many dollars as in the original graph, as in Figure 27c.

Beautiful, no?

Other Ways of Graphing Badly

The information in a graph is often made difficult to read through the principle of Alabama first. That is, the list of items in Figure 28a shows the life expectancies in a variety of nations by gender in alphabetical order. It's hard to see much of anything in the graph except that women live longer than men in all countries.

FIG. 28a   Life Expectancy at Birth, 1975

Women	Age	Men
Sweden	78	
France, US, Japan, Canada	77	
Finland, Austria, UK	76	
USSR, Germany	75	
	74	
	73	
	72	Sweden
	71	Japan
	70	
	69	Canada, UK, US, France
	68	Germany, Austria
	67	Finland
	66	
	65	
	64	
	63	
	62	USSR

Source: World Health Organization

FIG. 28b Life Expectancy at Birth, 1975

In Figure 28b, these data have been converted to what is known as a stem-and-leaf graph. The stem, in the middle, shows age. The leaves flare off to the sides of the stem and show the countries whose life expectancy fits one of those ages. Men's expectancies are shown on the right, women's on the left. This graph more dramatically shows how long women tend to outlive men and calls attention to the dramatically shorter life span of Russian men compared with all other nations in the graph.

Figure 28c, showing the most recent information on the same variable, is constructed from data on the World Health Organization's website.

Comparing Figures 28b and 28c, we see immediately an enormous improvement in life expectancy for everyone over the thirty-year period except in the Russian Federation. The life expectancy of Russian men declined four

Women	Age	Men
Japan	85	
France	84	
Sweden	83	
Austria, Canada, France, Germany	82	
United Kingdom	81	
United States	80	
	79	
	78	Sweden, Japan, Canada
	77	
	76	UK, Germany, France, Austria
	75	United States, Finland
	74	
	73	
Russian Federation	72	
	71	
	70	
	69	
	68	
	67	
	66	
	65	
	64	
	63	
	62	
	61	
	60	
	59	
	58	Russian Federation

Note: German and Russian Federation figures are not directly comparable in the two graphs because of the intervening reunification of Germany and the dissolution of the Soviet Union.

FIG. 28c   International Life Expectancies

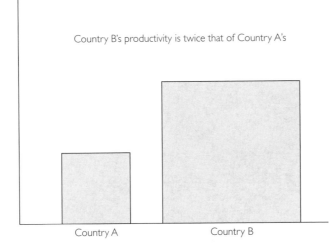

Country B's productivity is twice that of Country A's

Country A   Country B

FIG. 29   Productivity for Countries A and B

years, Russian women, three. In the earlier graph the women in no country had a life expectancy in the eighties; now all do, save Russia.

We earlier saw how simply taking a bunch of state-level SAT scores meant comparing the incomparable—each state offers a different-sized sample ranging from about 4 percent of its seniors to about 80 percent.

In the media, graphs often mislead when indicating the relative size of something. To make the graphs interesting, newspapers use, say, barrels to represent the size of oil production, or dollar signs to represent cost or gross domestic product or income. The distortion comes in when the media alter more than one dimension. Consider this in the simplest way. Let the boxes in Figure 29 represent countries, and let country B produce twice as much of something as country A. The difference between the countries might well be shown as in Figure 29.

The length of box B is twice the length of box A. The height of box B is twice the height of box A. This means that the *area* of box B—to which the eye is immediately drawn—is four times the area of box A. We could, if it suited our purpose, increase the distortion by making the drawings three-dimensional. In such a case, box B would occupy eight times the volume of box A.

While pictorial distortions provide the most common ways in which graphs mislead, their verbal content can deceive as well. Consider Figure 30, from *Workforce 2000: Work and Workers for the Twenty-first Century* (Johnson

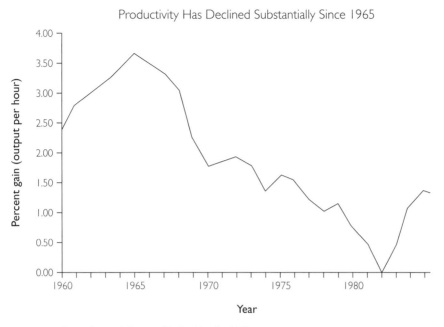

Productivity Has Declined Substantially Since 1965

FIG. 30 Productivity Graph

Source: Economic Report of the President, Jan. 1987

and Packer 1987). This graph shows that between 1965 and 1982 something fell rather dramatically. What was it?

The title says it's productivity: "Productivity Has Declined Substantially Since 1965." In a truly objective presentation, the word *substantially* would not be there—it's a word that tries to make up the reader's mind. But that is not the real problem. The vertical axis of Figure 30 reads "Percent Gain (output per hour)."

Well, percent gain is a rate, not a number. In order for productivity to fall, the percent gain would have to be negative, and it never is. For 1982 it comes very close to zero, but it would have to drop below the horizontal axis to be negative. Productivity has not fallen. The rate of productivity *gain* has fallen. From 1965 we became more productive more slowly, but we became more productive every year. (For the record, in the years subsequent to those shown on the graph, productivity gains improved.)

Again, learn to see through graphs.

4

Testing

A Major Source of Data—and Maybe Child Abuse

Were a Martian to drop in on America to explore our culture, it would soon phone home to tell other Red Planeteers that Americans think they can evaluate the entire educational enterprise using a single instrument, something called a test. Things have really gotten that crazy.

Let us for a moment consider a different perspective, a recent lament from a Belgian professor, Marc Romainville of the University of Namur. Romainville was especially perturbed at the use of tests to rank nations, but he bemoaned that ranking European nations on various variables was increasingly common: "Hit parades have been flourishing here for some years: the best schools, the world's best universities, the top performing research centers, etc. Some 30 years ago this sort of ranking would have produced a smile as we were of the view that the broad and long-term effects of education cannot be reduced to a few trivial indicators (test scores) and that every education system could be only validly understood by taking account of its history, its aims and the complexity of its structures" (2002, 86–89).

Sounds familiar to me, who grew up with phrases like "a sound mind in a healthy body," "a well-rounded person," and the notion that the true import and value of an education wouldn't be known until well after schooling itself had ended. We didn't call them "broad and long-term effects," but that's what people had in mind.

For many years, test-mad Asian nations (they make us look sane in comparison) scored the highest in international comparisons, but in fact, the highest-scoring nation in recent international comparisons is Finland. George W. Bush has said repeatedly that in order to know if children are learning, we must test. Finland is a one-word rebuttal to Bush's contention. Finland does not use tests at all to evaluate students, teachers, or schools. It maintains something similar to NAEP to take a periodic reading on the nation as a whole, but the nation at the pinnacle of the test-score heap doesn't use tests below the national level.

In America, in 2005, though, it is testing *uber alles.* As noted, NCLB uses nothing but tests to evaluate schools (it does tack on graduation rates as something of an afterthought). This crushing emphasis on test scores has produced some very bizarre events:

> In Bennett, Colorado, a father told school officials that he wanted to exempt his sixth-grade daughter from the state test. It labels children and schools and does nothing good for either, he said. You can do that, said the district superintendent, but your daughter will not be promoted to seventh grade (Rouse 2005).

> In Aberdeen, Washington, a fourth grader was working along fine on the state test until he encountered a writing prompt he didn't understand. His teacher told him repeatedly to keep working, but he said he couldn't (couldn't, not wouldn't). The teacher summoned the principal, who couldn't get him to answer. The principal summoned the mother, who couldn't get him to answer. The principal suspended him from school for a week for insubordination. The superintendent pleaded for help from the intermediate school district, the superintendent of which hired an outside consultant, who produced a thirty-page, four-thousand-dollar report that said, in perfect bureaucratese of course, the principal blew it (Horton 2005).

> In Texas, a teacher reported that her children who don't speak English well are taken each day from her regular class to be drilled on how to take the Texas state test. They miss art, music, and a library break (Bingham 2005).

> In Ohio a student was denied a diploma because he refused to take the Ohio Proficiency Tests. Writing in the *Athens News,* nongraduate John Wood called the tests "biased, irrelevant, and unnecessary." Wood observed that "in 13 years of testing, Ohio has failed to conduct any studies linking scores on the proficiency tests to college acceptance rates, college grades, income levels, incarceration rates,

dropout rates, scores on military recruiting tests, or any similar statistic" (Wood 2005).

➤ In Corpus Christi, Texas, Clydessa Coleman was in the hospital with
broken bones and damaged short-term memory from a car accident
that killed her eleven-year-old brother. Her high school asked for
waiver of the Texas state test. The Texas Education Agency refused.
An assistant principal went to the hospital to test her but, memory or
no, she had the good sense to refuse (Fernandez 2005).

➤ Many achievement tests come with instructions on what to do if a
child vomits on the answer sheet.

When the National Academy of Education reviewed a new plan for the
National Assessment of Educational Progress in 1987, it observed that

> Many of those personal qualities that we hold dear—resilience and
> courage in the face of stress, a sense of craft in our work, a commit-
> ment to justice and caring in our social relationships, a dedication to
> advancing the public good in communal life—are exceedingly dif-
> ficult to assess. And so, unfortunately, we are apt to measure what we
> can, and eventually come to value what is measured over what is left
> unmeasured. The shift is subtle and occurs gradually. (Alexander and
> James 1987)

Looking over this passage one day, I constructed a list of those "exceed-
ingly difficult to assess" personal characteristics:

creativity	self-discipline
critical thinking	leadership
resilience	civic-mindedness
motivation	courage
persistence	compassion
curiosity	resourcefulness
endurance	sense of beauty
reliability	sense of wonder
enthusiasm	sense of humor
empathy	honesty
self-awareness	integrity

At one point the list contained *cowardice*. Someone pointed out that it
was the only negative in the list. Cowardice had had a specific stimulus: stories on 9/11 of men shoving women aside to get on boats headed toward the

safety of New Jersey (courage entered the list that day as well). I realized that I could imagine an antonym for all of the qualities listed. The reader, I'm sure, can as well.

Like the qualities mentioned by the National Academy of Education, these are valued qualities, things that count in life much more than test scores and qualities for which tests do not or cannot exist or qualities for which tests are only seldom used (e.g., creativity and critical thinking).

When the stories of abuse at Abu Ghraib prison emerged, a few media articles harkened back to Harvard psychologist Stanley Milgram's experiments in the 1960s. When the subjects in Milgram's situation arrived, Milgram complained his research assistant had not shown up and pressed them into duty as such. He instructed them to administer shocks to a person visible in another room, strapped in a chair and wearing electrodes. The research, said Milgram, was about the effect of punishment on learning.

The apparatus actually delivered no shocks. The man strapped in the chair was a trained, paid actor. A scale painted on the apparatus, though, indicated that the shocks could vary from 15 to 450 volts. An area near the 450-volt mark was painted red with the word *Danger* above the paint. The new "research assistant" received a real 45-volt jolt to experience what it felt like.

When the shock level reached 75 volts, the man in the chair grunted; at 120 volts, he complained loudly; at 150 volts he demanded to be released from the experiment; his protests became more vehement and emotional until, at 285 volts, he emitted only agonized screams. Soon thereafter he fell totally silent.

The stranger in the white coat insisted that the experiment continue and, despite the strapped-down man's obvious agony, 60 percent of those enlisted into the experiment continued until the machine registered 450 volts. How, I wonder, did these 60 percent differ from the 40 percent who refused at some point to continue? I doubt that test scores would have predicted who would and would not yield to the authority of the man in the white coat.

Lest you think that Milgram was some kind of nut for conducting such an experiment, let me explain. In 1960 Israelis captured Adolph Eichmann in Argentina and put him on trial in Israel. During World War II Eichmann had served as the Nazis' transportation administrator, arranging the logistics of the trains hauling some 5 million Jews to concentration camps during World War II. Popular opinion in the United States, and perhaps elsewhere, held that Eichmann must be some kind of monster, a Jew-hating psychopath. No normal human being could oversee so much death. Eichmann said he was just doing his job, just following orders.

Philosopher Hannah Arendt, reporting in *The New Yorker,* agreed, saying she could find no indication of anti-Semitism or psychological damage in him. In her 1963 book *Eichmann in Jerusalem,* she put forth a theory of "the banality of evil." Anyone, she argued, under the right circumstances and with the right incentives could become an Eichmann.

How would one test such a theory? What kind of data could one possibly collect that would bear on it? Obviously, it would be too dangerous to society to attempt to create real Eichmanns. Milgram's experiment tried to test Arendt's theory on a small, nonlethal scale. The willingness of people to dispense pain when ordered to do so by a previously total stranger was considered evidence that Arendt was right. Eichmann was hanged in June 1962.

Back to testing.

Alas, the current abuse will go on for a while. I can only hope that some time in the future we will look back on this test-crazed era and ask, "What were we *thinking*?"

In the meantime, because tests abound, it's wise to know something about them. Unfortunately, I see educators who know little or nothing about tests attacking them all the time. These people are vulnerable to counterattacks by people who do know something about tests. Those who argue against tests in ignorance can be made to look very foolish by those who have a working knowledge of the field. If you don't want to be duped by the flow of data issuing forth from tests, you need to know something about what tests are and are not, what they can do and what they cannot.

In the current climate, and under the No Child Left Behind law, teachers and administrators can have their competence judged by test scores and can lose their jobs if the test scores come up short. Under state laws, teachers and administrators might get promoted or terminated because of test scores. Or they could get a bonus—in Birmingham, Alabama, 522 presumably low-scoring students were expelled from school just before the administration of the state test. The teacher who called public attention to this act was fired, but the test scores rose, so the superintendent received a bonus, as specified in his contract.

Chief among the uses of test scores these days is the measurement of adequate yearly progress—defined entirely by test scores—under NCLB. Because there is so much misunderstanding about how this law works, what it does and does not require, what sanctions it does or does not administer, I'll take some space to describe its principal features in reference to testing.

On October 3, 2001, the executive directors of many professional education organizations met to decide if they could support the education bill drafted by President Bush's staff and advisers. Only the American Association of School Administrators had the courage to oppose it. The remainder said merely that they could not support it. About the same time, the National Conference of State Legislatures also voiced opposition. A conference committee that was convened to reconcile the House and Senate versions of the bill reached agreement in December 2001. Bush signed the bill on January 8, 2002.

A November 2001 article in the *Washington Monthly* by journalist Thomas Toch succinctly captured the problems with the law: "[It] hurts the nation's students more than it helps them; promotes lower rather than higher standards; misleads the public about school performance; pushes teachers out of schools where they are most needed; and drives down the level of instruction in many classrooms" (2001). Toch, writing before NCLB became law, was prophetic.

Quite an accomplishment for one law and the education president.

NCLB required that each state establish a baseline of achievement—measured in test scores—and develop a plan to make adequate yearly progress (AYP) until, by the year 2013–14, 100 percent of each school's students had reached "proficient" in reading and math. Each state uniquely defined *proficient.*

NCLB mandates that schools test all students in grades 3–8 and in one grade in high school in reading and math. Beginning in 2007, testing in science in some grades will be added. In 2005, President Bush proposed adding more high school grades and Secretary of Education Margaret Spellings proposed adding more subjects. Neither proposal was received with any enthusiasm except, perhaps, by state governors, who collectively have a high school reform initiative in progress.

Schools must report not only their aggregate test scores but the scores of various subgroups. The subgroups were formed by

subject tested

grade

ethnicity

socioeconomic status

special education status

English language learner status

migrant status

percent tested (95 percent required for each subgroup)

Not all categories apply to all schools. States established a minimum size for reporting NCLB results, and this exempted a number of schools for some categories. For example, the minimum reporting size in Virginia is fifty. This means that 48 percent of Virginia's schools do not have to report results for different ethnicities and 78 percent do not have to report for students learning English. Most schools ended up with thirty-seven subgroups. If any subgroup failed to make AYP, the entire school was labeled "in need of improvement," a phrase that virtually no one used. "Failed school" was the common designation given by both educators and the media. A school in need of improvement was put on a watch list and had to develop a plan to improve.

If a school fails to make AYP for two consecutive years, the school must offer all students in the school the option of transferring to a "successful" school in the same district. If not all students could be accommodated through choice, the law mandates that the choice option be given first to the "neediest" students, those with the lowest test scores. The sending school bears the cost of any transportation. If that school later achieves AYP, it no longer has to pay for transportation, but students who had transferred do not have to return.

This requirement to date has been something of a farce. In New York City in 2003–4, some three hundred thousand students were eligible to transfer and about eight thousand did. Those eight thousand caused so many complaints from the principals at the receiving schools that in 2004–5 the city thumbed its nose at the law and limited the transfers to only one thousand. In rural areas there might well be no other schools in the district (the law limits choice to within-district transfers), or acting on the choice option might require an hours-long ride each way. In parts of Alaska and Hawaii it sometimes necessitates an airplane ride.

And, choice doesn't seem to be working. Few studies have been conducted, but it appears that students who transfer do no better than matched students who don't transfer—but they do end up in the principal's office more often (Kahn 2005).

If a school fails to make AYP for three consecutive years, it has to offer all low-income students in the school supplemental educational services (SES) such as tutoring outside the regular school day. A U.S. Department of Education ruling initially forbade *districts* that were themselves in need of improvement to offer the services. They had to turn to other institutions, mostly private, for-profit companies. The for-profit companies, however, could hire teachers from the failing districts to provide SES. Successful districts could employ their own teachers. Potentially, the SES provision could send more than $2 billion a year from the federal government through states and districts and into private coffers. Thus far, though, most eligible students are not receiving services. Perhaps for this reason, the department has softened its stand about forbidding teachers in failing districts to provide SES.

At this point in time, no schools are threatened with the fourth- and fifth-year sanctions unless they're in states that appended NCLB onto an ongoing state accountability program where the clock was already running (California, Colorado, Texas, and Michigan, for example). But, for the sake of completeness, here are sanctions schools might face next year or the year after.

If a school fails to make AYP for four consecutive years, it must choose from a variety of corrective actions that include adopting a new curriculum, replacing staff relevant to the failure, appointing outside experts, extending the school day or school year, or restructuring the organization.

After five consecutive years of failing to make AYP, a school can choose to open as a charter school, replace all or most staff, or contract with an outside entity to run the school.

All of these things happen or not based solely on changes in test scores. I wonder what kind of a look *that* would put on Professeur Romainville's face.

There are many other aspects of NCLB—the law is 1,100 pages long—but they have to do with highly qualified teachers, state and local report cards, and other features besides tests.

Some Facts About Tests

It seems appropriate as we start to learn about tests to see what you already know:

A Pop Quiz About Tests

Answer T (true) or F (false) to all questions.

1. T   F   If a school district's high school graduates do not all read at grade level, the district is not doing its job of educating the students.

2. T F If the average total SAT score at the university you most want to attend is 1100 and your total SAT score is only 1040, you shouldn't bother to apply.

3. T F If Mrs. Smith's students have lower scores than Mrs. Jones' students in the same grade of the same school, Mrs. Smith is not as good a teacher as Mrs. Jones.

4. T F If a school adopts a new curriculum and test scores fall, the new curriculum is inferior to the old curriculum.

5. T F The scores on a test naturally fall along a normal—bell-shaped—curve.

6. T F If students using curriculum A score significantly higher on a test than students using curriculum B, curriculum A is the better curriculum.

7. T F A fourth-grade student reading at the seventh-grade level should be promoted to the seventh grade, at least for reading instruction.

8. T F The SAT is a "common yardstick," meaning that two students from different states with the same score have the same potential for success in college.

9. T F If a child scores at the sixty-third percentile one year but falls to the fifty-seventh percentile the next year, something is wrong. Either the child isn't trying or the second year's teacher is not as effective.

10. T F Research indicates that IQ is 80 percent inherited.

11. T F If students can pass a test by getting 50 percent of the items right, the standards for passing are too low.

12. T F American students score lower on tests of mathematics and science than students in a number of other nations. This threatens our ability to compete in the global marketplace.

13. T F If one student scores at the forty-fifth percentile and another student scores at the nintieth percentile, the second student has scored twice as well as the first student.

The correct answer to all items is false.

Because the questions all reflect commonly held beliefs, I need to take some time to explain why each is false.

1. If a school district's high school graduates do not all read at grade level, the district is not doing its job of educating the students.

Most tests define *grade level* as the score of the average (median) child in a given grade. For a particular school, the Lake Wobegon effect could occur and all children could be above grade level. This effect, named for Garrison Keillor's mythical town where "all the women are strong, all the men are good-looking, and all the children are above average," can be seen in some affluent schools. But nationally, half of all students on most tests are, by definition, below average—that is, below grade level.

It is possible that the confusion about grade level has increased recently or will increase. Former Secretary of Education Rod Paige and current Secretary of Education Margaret Spellings are both on record as saying NCLB requires children to read at grade level. NCLB requires no such thing. It requires all students be proficient and leaves it to each state to specify what *proficient* means. Some observers, uncomfortable that fifty unique definitions of *proficient* mean that the states cannot be compared one with another, have proposed a common measure, namely, NAEP. Using NAEP in this way would be a disaster. The catastrophe that would occur is described on pages 147–151.

It is also *possible* that we could, by employing experts in various fields, establish skills that *all* children at a given grade could exhibit. Then we could determine if all children in a particular school scored at grade level. Such a determination would likely be an exercise in futility, though, and the level that constituted grade level would be quite low. Think of children's height and weight and the range these variables show from kid to kid. We could specify that all third graders must stand X inches tall, but the X would have to be a pretty short kid.

2. If the average total SAT score at the university you most want to attend is 1100 and your total SAT score is only 1040, you shouldn't bother to apply.

When colleges report their average SAT, such as 1100, that average is almost always the median score, meaning that half of the students attending the school scored above 1100 and half scored below. A score of 1040 is probably much less than a standard deviation below average and might well be acceptable. Besides, the SAT is only one factor in the admissions decision process. When Mount Holyoke abandoned the SAT a few years ago, the media gave the decision wide coverage, but even before the school dropped the

SAT, that test accounted only for 10 percent of what went into Holyoke's decision formula.

The question as phrased reflects a common myth: that all applicants to a college compete against all other applicants. But colleges tend to examine, and fill, certain categories. If they didn't, there would be no athletic programs or fine arts or performing arts programs. People with talents in the various arts often do not do well on paper-and-pencil tests. As Isadora Duncan famously said, "If I could *tell* you, I wouldn't have to dance."

Colleges do want high SAT scores in order to liberate money from alumni and impress future applicants, but they also want the well-rounded kid. If you are a "legacy"—if one or both of your parents attended the college—you have a better chance than others with the same score, and your chances greatly improve if you can attend as a "paying guest," that is, if your family can cover the expenses without recourse to a scholarship or a loan. Social conscience used to exist as an admissions category, but that has diminished under recent anti–affirmative action rulings.

3. If Mrs. Smith's students have lower scores than Mrs. Jones' students in the same school, Mrs. Smith is not as good a teacher as Mrs. Jones.

There are many possible reasons that the two classes have different test scores. It could be a random fluctuation. No test covers everything that a teacher covers. It could be that Mrs. Smith doesn't emphasize material covered by the test as much as Mrs. Jones. It could be Mrs. Jones tries harder to motivate students to do well on tests than Mrs. Smith. Or Mrs. Smith might be a newer teacher. Teacher experience counts. And veteran teachers are often assigned to or get to choose high-achieving classes.

4. If a school adopts a new curriculum and test scores fall, the new curriculum is inferior to the old curriculum.

The new curriculum might not match the test as well as the old curriculum. We tend to think in terms of reading is reading and mathematics is mathematics, but tests test specific aspects of reading and math. If American elementary students today took a mathematics achievement test from the late 1960s, they'd do quite poorly. Their performance wouldn't necessarily reflect low achievement, but rather a lack of familiarity with specific concepts on the test: In the 1960s some mathematicians felt that set theory was the royal road to learning mathematics, and terms like *ordinality, null set,* and *intersection of sets* filled the textbooks and showed up on the tests. Set theory is not so popular today and a test using the language of set theory would confuse today's students.

5. The scores on a test naturally fall along a normal—bell-shaped—curve.

Many tests will generate a bell-shaped curve, but often such a curve is forced on the data by the test maker, who chooses items that have certain statistical properties. But there is no necessity to this. As a teaching assistant at Stanford, I gave quizzes where most students got most items right and their scores piled up at the high end of the range. That is, on a ten-item quiz, most students would get eight, nine, or ten questions right. The quizzes were important, the students were bright and ambitious, and the students knew that we were supposed to grade on a pretty stiff curve (we were constantly in trouble with the administration for handing out too many As).

6. If students using curriculum A score significantly higher on a test than students using curriculum B, curriculum A is the better curriculum.

A statistically significant difference might have no or only small practical implications. Recall that statistical significance tells us only how likely it is that a difference between groups as large as the one we found could have happened by chance. Judgment is always required when making a practical decision about, say, adopting a new curriculum. If we had an experiment where kids studying under curriculum A scored significantly higher than kids studying under curriculum B at the .05 level, would we opt for curriculum A? What if curriculum A cost twice as much as curriculum B? Or if it required many more hours of teacher time for professional development? Or if the teachers hated it?

7. A fourth-grade student reading at the seventh-grade level should be promoted to the seventh grade, at least for reading instruction.

The fourth-grade student with a reading grade equivalent of seventh grade is not reading at the seventh-grade level. She has the same score as an average seventh grader would have *reading fourth-grade material.* In fact, this seventh-grade level is a statistical extrapolation—no seventh graders took the fourth-grade test. To give many other grades the fourth-grade test would be prohibitively expensive for a test publisher. Some third graders and some fifth graders do take the fourth-grade test and the developer extrapolates these data to see how second graders or sixth and seventh graders would have done.

8. The SAT is a "common yardstick," meaning that two students from different states with the same score have the same potential for success in college.

One of the underpinnings of any standardized test is that, *because* it is standardized, it treats all students the same. Thus, a student from South Succotash High with a 600 SAT is equivalent to a student from an elite private school with a 600 SAT. In theory. But consider two students. On the one hand, we have a student who comes from a well-educated, affluent family, attends a private, college-preparatory high school, and gets an SAT verbal of 600. On the other hand, we have a student who comes from an impoverished inner-city neighborhood, attends a public school with a small library, has no quiet place to study at home, and works to help the family make ends meet. This student also gets an SAT verbal of 600.

The myth of the common yardstick says these two students are academically equivalent. A lot of people would disagree. Ironically, some would disagree in different directions. A statistician would hold that the low-income student is less likely to succeed in college because of all the risk factors associated with his life. A college admissions officer, though, might well be impressed by that student's tenacity and ability to overcome obstacles.

Another ringer lies in the phrase *same potential for success.* Success in college depends on many factors—the high school curriculum taken, success in that curriculum, motivation, perseverance, and . . . luck.

9. If a child scores at the sixty-third percentile one year but falls to the fifty-seventh percentile the next year, something is wrong. Either the child isn't trying or the second year's teacher is not as effective.

I know of no published data that bear on this conclusion directly. Testing companies wouldn't go looking for it because instability in test scores would be an embarrassment. Some years ago, though, I examined scores of students over a four-year period in an elementary school that had low student mobility. Looking at the individual scores over that period, I found most students bouncing around a range of some twenty-five percentile ranks. That is, a student who got 62 one year might have other scores as high as 75 and as low as 50 in other years. Students above the ninety-fifth percentile on a test varied less. Students at the ninety-ninth percentile and students below the tenth percentile varied very little.

It is possible that the material in the second year was more difficult for the child. For me, nothing in high school was easier than chemistry. Physics, on the other hand, was a black hole.

10. Research indicates that IQ is 80 percent inherited.

Researchers vary greatly in how much they think genes and/or environment influence IQ. Recent work in a field called epigenetic analysis finds environmental influences can be subtle, yet powerful, even for identical twins, especially those who spend long periods apart.

11. If students can pass a test by getting 50 percent of the items right, the standards for passing are too low.

I am rather amazed at how many people believe this. Some years ago, the state superintendent of schools in Virginia wanted to set the passing score on the state's minimum competency at 60 percent correct simply because when he was in school, 60 was the minimum score for a D. Others argued that since it was a minimum competency test the passing score should be 100 percent correct. See the discussion on setting a passing score on pages 128–131.

Over the years, I have seen statements from school board members, state legislators, and a variety of others decrying a test as too easy because kids needed to get only half the items right to pass. This is silly. If you can pass a test by getting 50 percent of the items right, it might well mean that it's a very hard test (it could also be a bad test). In fact, on tests such as the TerraNova or the SAT10, only about half the students get any given item right. By design. We'll explain why this design exists later. Right now it suffices to note that the passing score and the difficulty of the test—the degree to which it reflects high standards—are quite independent of each other.

12. American students score lower on tests of mathematics and science than students in a number of other nations. This threatens our ability to compete in the global marketplace.

Tests have become so important in the eyes of groups like the Business Roundtable and some parents that the groups have lost all perspective on how important tests really are. American students actually do better in the international comparisons than critics would have you believe. In the most recent tests of mathematics and science, they finished in the middle among thirty-five or so countries, and in reading tests they did much better.

But tests are only one element, and a small one, in global competitiveness. Want a really important factor? Roads. Or rails or shipping or airlines. Or how about water—both to drink and to transport goods—or telephones or reliable, cheap access to the Internet, the dozens of variables that go into the single concept infrastructure? We got a glimpse of the importance of infrastructure in 2005 when much of it was wiped out in Hurricanes Katrina and Rita. Or how about AIDS or malaria? Sick people are not productive workers. Or how about a country with a government that strives mostly to keep power for itself? With a government that's interested in competition and the welfare of the people, Zimbabwe would be Africa's breadbasket. As it is, most people in Zimbabwe are dead before they turn forty.

The World Economic Forum, in Davos, Switzerland, annually ranks 117 nations on global competitiveness. It uses, literally, hundreds of variables collected into twelve factors it calls the Twelve Pillars of Competitiveness. Education is only one part of one pillar. In its *Global Competitiveness Report, 2004–2005.* the World Economic Forum ranked the United States the most competitive economy in the world.

(Someone in the public information office at the WEF messed up, and press releases for the 2004–5 and 2005–6 rankings announced that Finland was the most competitive economy. However, Finland's number one ranking was for the Growth Competitiveness Index, which is the WEF's assessment of a nation's potential for sustained economic growth. On this, the United States ranked second. But on the overall Global Competitiveness Ranking, the United States came in first.)

Let's be clear about this: *Education* is important to a nation's competitiveness. Vitally important. But, *given* education, test-score differences among developed nations are trivial. What, after all, does it mean to be a developed country? Well, for one thing it means to have an established, mature educational system from an early age through postdoctoral studies.

13. If one student scores at the forty-fifth percentile and another student scores at the ninetieth percentile, the second student has scored twice as well as the first student.

We can't use percentile ranks with statements like "twice as good" or "33 percent better." When we use percentiles, or temperature, or length, we are using a type of scale. Percentiles make up what is called an ordinal scale—they're like house numbers. We know that 406 South Elm Street is farther south than 402 South Elm Street, but we don't know how much farther. Maybe these addresses are on big lots, or maybe they're row houses, or maybe 406 is a half mile down the road from 402. We can't tell from the numbers. We'll talk more about this in the section on scales on pages 156–157.

There might be more or less than twice the "psychological distance" (a concept I just invented) between the forty-fifth percentile and the ninetieth. For instance, a student at the forty-fifth percentile of an IQ test would have an IQ of about 97. One at the ninetieth percentile would score an IQ of 120.

The Rise of Testing

If our little Martian friend had wafted down in, say, 1963, it would have had a much different take on America's reliance on tests. A little more than forty years ago, testing counted for little. In the early 1960s, the only people interested in SAT scores were college applicants and their parents, high school counselors, and college admissions officers. The decline in the SAT scores began in 1963 and didn't come to public attention until 1976.

In 1963, Commissioner of Education Francis Keppel and educator Ralph Tyler were just beginning to talk about constructing a test that Tyler developed into the National Assessment of Educational Progress. No international comparisons indicated how American students stacked up against those in other nations. No one in 1963 would have dreamed of giving children a readiness test to see if they were ready for kindergarten. Most states did not have a state testing program until well into the 1970s. Minimum competency tests did not arrive until the late 1970s, except in Denver, which developed one in 1958 at the behest of businessmen who then ignored it. In 1978, a reporter from the *Racine Journal Times* was investigating the impact of minimum competency tests, and when he visited Denver, he checked in with the chief personnel officer at Mountain Bell, then the area's largest employer. "Have you noticed any improvement in Denver high school graduates since the installation of the minimum competency test? he asked. "What minimum competency test?" she asked back. Mountain Bell administered its own (Frahm 1979).

Schools had taken a beating from critics in the 1950s and the Soviet Union's launch of Sputnik in October 1957 simply proved to those critics that they had been right all along. But their proposed solutions did not lie in tests. They lay in curriculum. Professors of mathematics and sciences expended vast amounts of energy to modernize and improve curricula (not all of the innovations were improvements, as witness the disaster of the New Math).

In the late 1960s to mid-1970s tests took on increasing importance. Partly this resulted from an unfortunate disconnect between the psychometric community and the teaching profession. Historically, teachers have never considered standardized, multiple-choice tests as valid indicators of what they hoped to accomplish in classrooms. Historically, psychometricians, although experimenting with various item formats, were largely satisfied with their products, and the multiple-choice format, the fastest and cheapest, came to virtually exclude all others (other formats had something of a revival in the 1980s).

This disconnect was harmless as long as testing had little to do with the evaluation of programs, teachers, or schools. But in 1965, the first Elementary and Secondary Education Act required that programs be evaluated to determine if they had improved matters. When people looked around for instruments to use in the evaluations, what they found was, mostly, tests.

In the mid-1970s the back-to-basics and minimum competency testing movements percolated through the states. Newspapers began reporting test-score results for districts in their markets. The results appeared in box-score fashion and the suburbs invariably scored higher than the cities they surrounded.

The importance and visibility of tests increased dramatically with the College Board's 1976 publication *On Further Examination* and 1983's *A Nation at Risk*. The College Board set out to find reasons for the then fourteen-year decline in SAT scores. And did it find reasons! One background document simply listed all of the hypotheses put forward to explain the fall. The paper listed seventy-four hypotheses dealing with demographic changes, culture, family, curriculum, teacher quality, and on and on.

In its report, the board attributed most of the decline to changes in who was taking the test: more women, more minorities, more students from low-income families, more students with mediocre high school records. The press and the general public didn't see it that way: they concluded that American high schools had failed.

A Nation at Risk built on that conclusion. As noted earlier, after its cold warrior introduction about "a rising tide of mediocrity," the booklet listed thirteen indicators of the risk. Twelve of them dealt directly with test scores and the thirteenth did so indirectly. All pertained to high schools, and the thirteenth presented complaints from business and industry about how much money they had to spend on remedial education. *Risk* arrived at the height of the trend (some would say madness) to make high school diplomas contingent on passing a minimum competency test. *Minimum* competency is not good enough, said the authors of *Risk.* "Our Nation's people and its schools and colleges must be committed to achieving excellence" (National Commission on Excellence in Education 1983, 12–13).

Risk fretted that other nations, those with higher test scores, would outstrip us economically. When the Soviets launched Sputnik, the perceived threat was that if the schools didn't shape up, the Russians might gain spaceflight and weapons superiority and vaporize us off the planet. Now, according to the authors of *Risk,* the threat was more that our friends, especially Germany, Japan, and South Korea, would take away our markets: "If only to keep and improve on the slim competitive advantage we still retain in world markets, we must dedicate our selves to the reform of our educational system" (7). This was silly but widely accepted then and still silly and widely accepted now.

Educational quality was thereafter linked to tests. *High standards* became the catchphrase of the day. We needed tests to measure how well the students were attaining the standards.

But there is more to the rise of testing—or less, depending on your perspective—than just a few public documents, even if one of them, *A Nation at Risk,* galvanized public attention to the schools. Put simply, people lost faith in the achievement information flowing from schools. More than other nationalities, Americans have always had great faith in science and technology—in numbers!—to show what's *really* happening. Some friends of mine, visiting Austria, asked an Austrian teacher about tests and whether she used them to learn how well her students read. She looked insulted. "Nothing can know these students better than I can." Austrians believe this. Many Americans do not. Americans want numbers and they want those numbers to offer the kind of "objective," "scientific" proof they *think* they get from tests. As a consequence, in the last score of years, testing has metastasized.

The Nature of Standardized Tests

Just what constitutes a standardized test? A test is standardized if

> the questions are the same for everyone
> the format of the questions is the same for everyone
> the instructions given the students are the same for everyone
> the time allotted to take the test is the same for everyone
> the tests are usually administered to a group of students

➤ the items on the test have known statistical properties, especially in terms of the proportion of test takers who get each item right

Although standardized tests are often contrasted against teacher-made tests, many if not most teacher-made tests share many of the above characteristics. However, teachers usually don't have information about the statistical properties of individual items.

There *are* deviations from the above that serve to unstandardize some aspects of a test. For instance, there is growing use of what psychometricians call *computerized adaptive tests.* Students take these tests using a computer and, increasingly, online. All students start out on the same questions, but as a student answers the questions, the questions she gets next depend in part on how well she has performed on previous questions. Students getting all questions right will advance to more difficult questions and, if they continue to get all questions right, more difficult questions still. Students having trouble at a particular level of questions will receive easier questions. The computer adapts to the students' performance, hence the name computerized adaptive testing.

Similarly, students receiving certain types of special education services might get more time to finish or might qualify for other modifications such as large print or oral presentation of questions. Some state accountability tests are not timed.

. While most tests test students in groups, some tests, such as some IQ tests, are taken by individuals. In such cases, the test administrators themselves are standardized—they must be trained how to administer the various parts of the test. While teachers can administer the standardized tests given to groups using the instructor's manual supplied by the publisher, those who administer individual tests must know those tests intimately. They are given some flexibility in sequencing questions and what would constitute a correct answer. But even here, they must be trained to recognize what is an allowable deviation from the usual sequence.

I came on one of my favorite illustrations of deviations in answers while touring Ellis Island. One building there contains a room devoted to the intelligence tests that would-be immigrants sat for as the inspectors determined whether or not they would be allowed in. The example on one wall asked this question:

Do you wash stairs from the top or from the bottom?

The 1917 answer of Polish hopeful Nadine Patkoff: "I don't go to America to wash stairs."

I don't know how the test administrator scored this answer, but the plaque does say that Patkoff was admitted. This story actually highlights an important aspect of tests that is largely overlooked: face validity. Face validity reflects the degree to which those taking the test take it seriously. Children in elementary grades attribute face validity to most tests, but as they get older, they have less and less faith that the tests are accurate or that they measure the students' important skills and abilities.

Construction of a Standardized Test

Until recently, the most common type of standardized test was a norm-referenced test, or NRT. Examples of norm-referenced tests are the Iowa Tests of Basic Skills, the TerraNova, the Stanford Achievement Test, tenth edition (SAT10), the California Achievement Test, the Metropolitan Achievement Test, and the Comprehensive Tests of Basic Skills.

The techniques for constructing such tests are themselves quite standardized. Publishers peruse the most commonly used textbooks and other classroom materials and develop questions that reflect the common instructional goals found in these materials. Curriculum specialists then rate the questions for "content validity"—a judgment as to whether the question really measured what it claimed to measure.

The judgment of content validity is more subtle and more important than it might seem at first glance. As Richard Rothstein observes in the following passage, while items might be aligned with a learning standard and thus measure its content, they might well not assess the full scope of the standard:

> Consider a typical elementary school reading standard, common in many states, that expects children to be able to identify both the main idea and the supporting details in a passage. There is nothing wrong with such a standard. If state tests actually assessed it, there would be nothing wrong with teachers "teaching to the test." But in actuality, students are more likely to find questions on state tests that simply require identification of details, not the main idea. For example, a passage about Christopher Columbus might ask pupils to identify his ships' names without asking if they understood that, by

sailing west, he planned to confirm that the world was spherical. In math, a typical middle-school geometry standard expects students to be able to measure various figures and shapes, like triangles, squares, prisms and cones. Again, that is an appropriate standard and the teachers should prepare students for a test that assessed it. But, in actuality, students are more likely to find questions on state tests that ask only for measurement of the simpler forms, like triangles and squares. It is not unusual to find states claiming that they have "aligned" such tests with their high standards when they have done nothing of the kind (2004, 91).

> **Principle of Data Interpretation:** *Make certain that any test aligned with a standard comprehensively tests the material called for by the standard.*

With questions in hand, the test developer would then administer them to groups of people to see if the items "behaved properly." Proper behavior in a test question is a matter of statistical properties. An item that everyone gets right or everyone gets wrong is behaving badly; if everyone gets an item right, you can't tell anything about the skills of different people. And, as we saw in the little section on point biserial correlations, items that high scorers get wrong and low scorers get right are not behaving properly.

Once the developer has assembled a collection of nicely behaved questions, the developer administers them to a large number of people around the country. The test developer will try to arrange that this large number represents the nation. That is, those taking the test should represent the appropriate mixture in each grade of affluent, middle-class, and poor children, rural, urban, and suburban children, and children of various ethnicities. This large group of people is referred to as the national norming sample (*sample*, recall, because although we're testing lots of people, we're not testing everyone). The average score—median, fiftieth percentile—of all these children is called the national norm, and this gives the test its name, norm-referenced standardized test or, as it is usually abbreviated, NRT.

All scores are referenced to the performance of this norming group. If your fifth-grade child scores at the seventy-fifth percentile, you know that he outscored 75 percent of the fifth graders in the national norming sample (*not* outscored 75 percent of the people who took the test that year. If the test was normed in 2002 and your child takes it in 2005, your child's score and those of her peers are referenced to the 2002 norming sample, not to others taking the test in 2005).

This characteristic of NRTs, having the norm at the median, bothers some people because it means that, by definition, half of all students always fall below average. Some schools might have everyone above average, and some schools might have virtually everyone below average, but, nationally, 50 percent of the students will always be below average.

> **Principle of Data Interpretation:** *On a norm-referenced test, nationally, 50 percent of students are below average, by definition.*

What do NRTs test? As we saw in the answer to question 4 of the quiz, they test specific skills. Certainly there is some overlap among the major test publishers because there is some consistency across the nation in what is taught, especially in elementary schools. This leads to a major constraint on what NRTs can test: They must seek to test only materials that all children have been exposed to. To do otherwise would treat some children unfairly.

To do otherwise would also diminish the test publishers' treasuries. Many states have state-adopted tests. They typically put out a call for proposals from the publishers and award a contract to the company offering the test that seems best suited to the state and which is also often, but not always, the cheapest.

State requirements can influence the content of tests. For example, for many years the Iowa Tests of Basic Skills did not have a computation test. The developers of the ITBS felt that localities ought to have the freedom to determine how and when they taught various arithmetic computations. They also thought computation was the skill most easily skewed by endlessly drilling students in arithmetic operations. They are probably correct in this belief, meaning that it is hard to know what computation scores mean in the larger frame of things.

In 1976, though, Texas and California advised Riverside, the ITBS' publisher, that without a computation test the ITBS could not compete for adoption as their state test. As the two most populous states in the country, and as states with a higher proportion of young people than many other states, Texas and California represent two enormous contracts (the influence of these states in determining what gets into textbooks has been a source of debate and complaint for many years). So, Riverside yielded and added a computation test. Some years later, it arranged to make the computation test optional: states or districts that agreed with the test developers' philosophy could skip computation if they chose.

The need to test only skills commonly taught means that anything special about a school or a district will not likely find its way onto the test. Consider the curriculum at the Key School in Indianapolis. The Key School began life as a preK–6 public magnet school that chose students by lottery except that the ethnic makeup of the school had to mirror that of Indianapolis public schools generally. Since its founding in 1985 it has grown into a preK–12 institution. Its founders organized it around Howard Gardner's theory of multiple intelligences. Gardner had chided schools for concentrating on only two of the intelligences, verbal and quantitative. He had elevated musical, spatial, kinesthetic, interpersonal, and intrapersonal intelligences to the same levels as the first two.

Seeking to develop all intelligences, the teachers at Key teach all children to play a musical instrument. All learn a foreign language. There are activities to foster the interpersonal and intrapersonal intelligences. The Key School also offers minicourses the teachers call pods, which are not linked to Gardner's ideas. In pods, teachers teach about the things that interest them outside of school. The theory is that if the students see the teachers genuinely interested and enthusiastic about something and doing it in real life, they might get interested in it, too, or, at the least, get a feel for what true interest looks like. If my observations of children studying pods on Victorian architecture and pottery making are accurate, the theory works.

On Wednesday afternoons, the teachers retire to a staff room for planning and evaluation meetings. Planning might be for next week or next year. Volunteers take the students to the auditorium/gym, where some person or group from the larger community explain their jobs. Once when I visited, the kids heard paramedics and nurses explain their duties and the skills needed; another time a quartet from the Indianapolis Symphony talked about music and the history of their instruments and played some pieces. In the Q-and-A session that followed, the quartet was greatly impressed by the sophistication of the students' questions.

The Key School's day is long and both teachers and students leave tired, but you can sense from watching the kids that they enjoy being there. Their parents are happy with this school. Many education organizations have praised it and television news programs have featured it.

But teaching a musical instrument will not raise the school's score on the ITBS or any other NRT. The language of music is too specialized, and most elementary schools only offer band to a few students and not until third or fifth grade. Around the country, few children will know what a *glissando* or an *arpeggio* is or how to play *adagio*. So those words can't show up on the ITBS vocabulary tests. They can't even show up in reading passages unless the passage also defines them or makes them the focus of the passage—unknown words make reading passages harder to comprehend.

Knowing Spanish, the foreign language taught at the school, *might* help students one day figure out the meaning of an otherwise inscrutable SAT word if they can see the root word it contains, but that help is many years off. Spanish words or words from other languages might show up in a reading passage, but, again, they would have to be defined, discussed, or a focus within the passage, not reflect knowledge that kids could be expected to bring to the test.

Blowing away a visiting group of classical musicians might certainly impress visitors, but that won't improve the school's test scores, either. In terms of scoring high on Indiana's state test for accountability, the Key School would be better off spending the time on the state objectives. But that, of course, would betray wholly the reason the Key School exists.

> **Principle of Data Interpretation:** *A norm-referenced standardized achievement test must test only material that all children have had an opportunity to learn.*

> **Principle of Data Interpretation:** *Standardized norm-referenced tests will ignore and obscure anything that is unique about a school.*

The clause one size fits all has been rather much overused of late, but it certainly is appropriate when talking about standardized tests, especially nationally normed tests. The tests *must* be that way. Even the courts have said so.

In *Debra P. v. Turlington,* Florida students argued that the state could not withhold their diplomas if they failed the state's minimum competency test because in many instances the students had not had an opportunity to learn the material on the test. The court agreed and required the state to present evidence of such opportunity. It gave the state a few years to comply, but only after those few years could the state make a diploma contingent on passing the test.

Now, if a test could cover everything we want children to know, the condition of testing would be much improved. But that never happens. Most tests have only twenty-five to forty questions per subject and are timed. Virginia's Standards of Learning Tests are not timed and some use other than the multiple-choice format, but many objectives that are listed in the standards are never tested. They are not all tested, in part because to assess all objectives would make the tests unbearably long, but also because some objectives can be assessed only individually or by watching or listening to a student performance.

The preceding passages make a case for localized testing. It would be fine for the students at the Key School to have words like *arpeggio* on tests, and some could have *kiln,* or *mansard roof* as well, as these have been part of their curriculum at the school. But local assessments would not be backed up by statistics like *p* values or point biserials, so they tend not to count for much.

Standardized norm-referenced tests push us toward standardized kids.

> **Principle of Data Interpretation:** *Scores from standardized tests are meaningful only to the extent that we know that all students have had a chance to learn the material which the test tests.*

In at least one instance, testing kids on stuff they hadn't learned help made the United States look bad in an international comparison. In 1995, what was then known as the Third International Mathematics and Science Study (TIMSS) attempted to compare students in the last year of secondary school as well as in the more commonly tested grades, 4 and 8 (because the study is now conducted every four years, the word *Third* has been replaced by *Trends;* there have been TIMSS assessments in 1995, 1999, and 2003 with results reported the following year). *Final year of secondary school* was a term used quite deliberately because the people conducting the comparison knew that final year of secondary school meant different things in different countries. In some countries, secondary school is a three-year program; in others it's five years. In the United States, most students attend comprehensive high schools even though there is tracking to a greater or lesser degree within schools. In most other nations, students are tracked into specific programs: college bound, science and technology, arts and humanities, vocational, and so on.

When the U.S. Department of Education released the results at a press conference, it gave the impression that a peer-to-peer comparison had transpired: American seniors had been tested against seniors in other countries—an apples-to-apples comparison. Apples to aardvarks was more like it though. There were many differences among the countries in terms of how long secondary school had lasted, what students had learned, and how old the students were. American students apparently ranked quite low.

For the advanced mathematics and physics tests, nations were allowed to choose which students were appropriate to test. In advanced mathematics, we tested students who had completed calculus and those who had completed precalculus ("completed" because the tests were administered very close to the end of the school year, something of a problem in itself). When I asked why we included precalculus students, I was told by Larry Suter of the National Science Foundation, "Just to see how they'd do." Well, that's fine, but that should have been made clear to the media and it wasn't. How'd they do? They did awful. They scored fully one hundred points lower than American students who actually had calculus under their belts. Those who had taken calculus finished in the middle among the participating nations.

Criterion-Referenced Tests

Norm-referenced tests (NRTs) are not much in favor these days. They have given way to criterion-referenced tests (or CRTs) although the current crop of CRTs is not what the framers of the concept had in mind. Most states have developed sets of standards and tests that are at least somewhat aligned with them (only somewhat in part because, at least in the case of Virginia, some of the standards cannot be assessed with any kind of paper-and-pencil tests and so are not being assessed although all standards are supposedly equally important).

When the concept of CRT reappeared in the early 1960s (E. L. Thorndike had first talked about the concept around 1913), it generated a lot of excitement among many in the testing field. The idea of a CRT "totally destroyed the monopoly of norm-referenced tests that was held in many quarters," according to the late psychometrician Jason Millman (1994, 19).

So what is a criterion-referenced test? Robert Glaser invented the term and contended that for any clearly specified set of behaviors, we could imagine a continuum of achievement ranging from zero competence to conspicuous excellence. If the behavior was, say, ice-skating, zero competence might be "unable to stand on ice unassisted" and conspicuous excellence might be "completes triple Axel with perfect landing." In between these extremes would be a variety of performances all referenced to a clearly specified set of behaviors.

It's easy to see why people got excited. NRTs measure people against other people: how does one person or group of people stack up against another group of people, those who produced the national norm? CRTs promised to change that in two ways. First, CRTs would measure people along a continuum of achievement against specific criteria. Perhaps more exciting, CRTs would measure people against themselves: how their behavior changed as they moved along that continuum of achievement Glaser spoke about.

Alas, it did not work out as envisioned. It is not an accident that the previous example comes from ice-skating and not from education. The domains of education do not yield easily a clearly specified set of behaviors. Ice-skating is all behavior. We can observe it and a set of judges can agree, often unanimously, on how well the skater indeed performed the behaviors. It is not so easy to arrive at a clearly specified set of behaviors for what is taught in school. People even disagree on what a domain for measurement in education might contain: consider the math wars with some groups emphasizing computation and basic skills on the one hand but others wanting mathematics to emphasize the power of math and mathematical concepts.

In addition, education has to do with what goes on inside the head. Behaviorists have tried to infer these internal events (or to ignore them altogether) from overt behavior, but with only limited success. Perhaps advances in cognitive psychology through various brain-imaging techniques will one day permit us to have a sufficiently clear idea of what goes on in there, but that day is not here yet.

Finally, ice-skating involves a limited range of behavior. Education is both more general and more complex. Millman said, "I thought that if only educators could write good test specifications, explicitly stating what was and was not part of the content coverage, CRT's would be able to meet their promise. But I was wrong" (1994, 19).

Criterion-Referenced Versus Standards-Referenced Tests: Setting a Passing Score

What are often called CRTs these days are nothing like the CRTs that Glaser and Millman had in mind. They are more appropriately called standards-referenced tests. Some folk actually refer to them as politically referenced tests because so many have been brought into existence via political agendas, not educational concerns. With them has come a perplexity: people confuse *criterion* with *cut score* or *passing score.* Ask people to name the criterion on some state test and they will give you the cut score. That is certainly *a* criterion, the criterion for passing the test, but it is nothing like the clearly specified set of behaviors that people had in mind when CRTs first became popular. This criterion is simply a barrier that the students have to jump over.

Establishing the locus of that barrier by setting any passing score is an arbitrary process. One can only hope that it will be arbitrary in the sense of arbitration, not arbitrary in the sense of capricious. There are two generally accepted methods for setting a cut score, the modified Angoff method and the bookmark method. There are lots of technicalities in the actual procedures that we won't go into here, but setting a cut score is an important and potentially dangerous procedure, so you ought to know a little about how it's done.

The Angoff method is named for its creator, William Angoff. In this procedure, a committee, usually of twenty people, looks at each item on a test. Each committee member judges the odds that a "minimally competent or minimally qualified or minimally acceptable" person would get it right (sometimes they guess how many out of one hundred such people would get it right). The committee generally represents a range of expertise. If the questions are for, say, a mathematics test, the judges might consist of some middle school and high school math teachers, some math curriculum supervisors, some professors of mathematics education, and some people unaffiliated with the field of mathematics, perhaps parents or school board members.

Today the usual procedure is called a modified Angoff. The modification calls for a second round of judgments. After judges have made their decisions about how many minimally competent people will get an item right, they discuss their answers and provide rationales, especially if the judges have showed substantial disagreement. There is then a second round of judging the same item—people are given a chance to change their judgments if they choose to.

Adding up the judgments for each person and averaging them yields one cut score for the test per person, or twenty cut scores altogether. It is generally recommended that the cut score be set somewhere in the average range of twenty individual cut scores. In Virginia, though, the state board of education used the highest passing score anyone had recommended. It has subsequently and quietly lowered the passing score on a number of tests. Virginia is not unique in this respect although some states have been secretive about the changes for fear that admitting the arbitrariness of the cut score might undermine the test's and the board's credibility. Delaware might be unique in raising some cut scores and lowering others (Le 2005).

The Virginia board's action, though, serves to remind us that not only is setting a cut score not a scientific process, but it is a political process. The placement of the cut score depends, in part, on how much failure the public will tolerate. No state, to the best of my knowledge, has ever conducted a validity study of its passing scores. A component of such a study would be to inquire of colleges, employers, and perhaps the military if they have changed their opinions about the quality of students arriving at their gates since the tests were imposed. In fact, the Virginia Technical Advisory Committee to the state's Standards of Learning Program repeatedly urged the state to conduct such a study.[1] The state dissolved the committee. On page 103 I quoted high schooler John Wood, listing all of the analyses the state of Ohio should have done but hadn't to validate the Ohio Proficiency Tests.

A June 2005 analysis by the *Boston Globe* suggests states might be politically wise although ethically off base to avoid validity studies. The *Globe* found that in 2002, the last year before the Massachusetts high school diploma became contingent on passing a test, 39 percent of Massachusetts college freshmen required a remedial course in reading, writing, or mathematics. Three years after the diploma requirement was in place, the figure had dropped only 2 percent to 37 percent. In Boston, 86 percent of the class of 2003 passed the test, but of the 365 freshmen enrolling at Bunker Hill Community College, 62 percent required remedial reading and 89 percent required remedial math. "Basically we have not seen any change at all," said David Hartleb, president of Northern Essex Community College (Sacchetti 2005, A1).

> **Principle of Data Interpretation:** *Any attempt to set a passing score or a cut score on a test will be arbitrary. Ensure that it is arbitrary in the sense of arbitration, not in the sense of being capricious.*

In the bookmark standard-setting procedure judges see all of the items that are on a test and have some time to discuss what skills they call for. The

1. In fact, the TAC's recommendations were to evaluate the consequences of the entire program: Do students score higher on the SAT and NAEP? Have curricula narrowed? Are teachers satisfied with the program or are they fleeing the state or taking early retirement? Is the dropout rate changing? Does the program have a negative impact on minorities, special education students, or English language learners? And so on.

judges then receive a booklet containing all of the items, one to a page, but in this booklet the items are ordered from easiest to hardest (this information was obtained when the items were first tried out to see how they behaved). Judges discuss the items and then individually place a bookmark between the two items they think would separate a minimally qualified person from an unqualified person.

The judges could also be asked to place bookmarks where they think there is a dividing line between minimum and proficient or between proficient and advanced. As with Angoff, a round of discussion occurs during which judges can adjust their bookmarks if they choose. There might also be some "impact" data showing what proportion of test takers would not be judged minimally competent if the bookmark was placed at a certain point.

I have taken the time to discuss the cut-score-setting procedures because (1) it involves important decisions, (2) it is not magic, and (3) it is not objective science. As long as there are tests with consequences, there are judgments that must be made, and they too have consequences.

Performance Tests and Portfolios

During the 1980s and early 1990s renewed interest in performance tests was aroused. One of its proponents was Albert Shanker, president of the American Federation of Teachers. Shanker held up two examples from other fields: the tests represented by Boy Scout merit badges and the tests administered to his son while interning at the CIA—the Culinary Institute of America. The badges set out precisely what had to be done to earn them and specified criteria by which performance would be judged. In the same way, Shanker's son was evaluated by the concoctions he produced and the skills he displayed in the process of producing them.

Many politicians and some educators in those years were speaking in terms of "what our students should know and be able to do." It seemed like the "to do" part clearly required some kind of performance test.

The trend to use performance testing was halted by another trend, that toward standards-referenced state testing programs. Only one state, Maryland, was interested in a performance-based program that tested a sample of students. While sampling saves a great deal of money and time, naturally, scores do not arrive for all students. Maryland sampled enough students to give each *school* a score, but no one received individual student scores. Both parents and politicians pressed for programs that would test everyone.

Administering performance tests of any kind to all students would prove too expensive and so, as a state-level assessment, performance tests faded out. Some remain at the school level.

As an aside, I might mention that during this same time frame, people often spoke of "authentic assessment." It was never really clear what that phrase meant, although some took it to mean that testing with multiple-choice questions was inauthentic, requiring only the selection of the correct answer from a prearranged set of answers. Probably the meaning that came closest to consensus was that authentic assessment involved meaningful, real-world problems.

In the final section in this chapter, "The Future of Testing," I describe a type of test that might bring performance testing back to the fore, tests that seek to determine what people really know and how they actually learn.

International Tests

International tests are not a separate type of test, but they have assumed such visibility in recent years as indicators of nations' well-being and have been so misinterpreted in some quarters that we need to talk a bit about them.

The early attempts at international comparisons, in the 1960s, were marred by an inability of the organizations sponsoring the tests to control whom the various countries tested. The United States has a culture of public self-criticism and could be counted on to draw the appropriate representative sample. Some countries only tested groups that would make them look good.

By the '90s, most, but not all, of these problems had been attended to, especially at the most commonly tested grades, 4 and 8. Each country that participates provides a list of all its schools and some demographic descriptors for each school. A national probability sample is then drawn. Of course, most countries can't force the chosen schools to participate, so replacement schools have to be chosen as well. In some cases where many schools have declined to test students, questions have arisen about whether the replacement schools were as representative as those that opted out (schools that opt out are often those that would be predicted to score low).

The Hague-based International Association for the Evaluation of Educational Achievement—which somehow always gets abbreviated to IEA—conducts TIMSS. TIMSS assessments have taken place in 1995 in grades 4, 8, and the final year of secondary school, in 1999 in grade 8 only, and in 2003 in grades 4 and 8. The IEA also conducts assessments of reading each decade. Much of the psychometric work and data processing for the TIMSS reports takes place at Boston College (and much of the cost is borne by American taxpayers).

The other program is PISA, Program for International Student Assessment, operated by the Organization for Economic Cooperation and Development, headquartered in Paris. PISA tests fifteen-year-olds in reading, mathematics, and science, and each assessment emphasizes one of the three areas but also tests the other two. Most fifteen-year-olds are in the tenth grade but some students are in grades 8 and 9 (very few are in 11).

The two programs differ considerably. TIMSS uses only multiple-choice questions and the stems of its questions are quite short (the stem is the part of a question that presents the information or problem). PISA uses more open-ended questions and its stems are often long and discursive. As a consequence, while we can rest comfortably assured that TIMSS tests mathematics and science skills taught in schools, it is not at all clear what PISA tests. The long stems mean that students have to read a lot and therefore even questions that present mathematics problems or science experiments also measure students' reading skills—but the questions don't generate separate scores for reading.

PISA claims to test students' ability to apply what they've learned to new situations, but it also claims to assess information that students might have learned outside of school. I find these claims problematic because, of course, what students learn outside of school depends a lot on where that school is. Students whose schools are in rural Greece will likely learn quite different things outside of school, television and the Internet notwithstanding, than will students in Paris or Manhattan.

In fact, a researcher in England pointed out that a PISA question involving cars on racetracks had very different results for boys and girls and that these differences were heightened for rural girls versus urban boys. Boys did better than girls. Boys in more urbanized nations did much better than girls in more rural countries. To answer the question, the student needed to know something about the shapes of racetracks and how drivers employ acceleration and braking to negotiate a course.

Here are two sample questions from PISA, the first in math, the second in science, and my annotations.

Seal's Sleep

A seal has to breathe even if it is asleep in the water. Martin observed a seal for one hour. At the start of his observation, the seal was at the surface and took a breath. It then dove to the bottom of the sea and started to sleep. From the bottom it slowly floated to the surface in 8 minutes and took a breath again. In three minutes it was back at the bottom of the sea again. Martin noticed that this whole process was a very regular one.

After one hour the seal was a) at the bottom, b) on its way up, c) breathing, d) on its way down.

Obviously test takers have to play the testing game to some extent. For instance, they must assume that "very regular" means that it always takes exactly eight minutes to rise up, zero seconds to breathe, and exactly three minutes to dive. And, because it takes a sleek seal three minutes to get to the bottom of the sea, Martin obviously couldn't really see to that depth. One wonders how well children who have never seen a seal would fare.

Chocolate Diet

A newspaper article recounted the story of a 22-year-old student named Jessica, who has a "chocolate diet." She claims to remain healthy, and at a steady weight of 50 kg, whilst eating 90 bars of chocolate a week and cutting out all other food, apart from one "proper meal" every five days. A nutrition expert commented: I am surprised someone can live with a diet like this. Fats give her energy to live but she is not getting nearly enough vitamins. She could encounter serious health problems in later life.

In a book with nutritional values, the following data are applicable to the type of chocolate Jessica is eating all the time. Assume also that the bars of chocolate she eats have a weight of 100 grams.

Protein	Fats	Carbohydrates	Minerals		Vitamins			Total Energy
			calcium	iron	A	B	C	kJ
g	g	g						
5	32	61	50	4	—	0.20	—	2142

The nutrition expert said that Jessica ". . . is not getting nearly enough vitamins." One of those vitamins missing in chocolate is vitamin C. Perhaps she could compensate for her shortage of vitamin C by including a food that contains a high percentage of vitamin C in her "proper meal every five days." Here is a list of types of food:

1. fish 2. fruit 3. rice 4. vegetables

Which two types of food from this list would you recommend to Jessica in order to give her a chance to compensate for her vitamin C shortage?

A. 1 and 2, B. 1 and 3, C. 1 and 4, D. 2 and 3, E. 2 and 4, F. 3 and 4

Most of this item is irrelevant to the problem (a second question asks if all of the energy comes from fat). To get at the question's intent, which is, according to OECD, "demonstrating knowledge and understanding of science in life and health," it would seem the following stem would do as well: "The doctor tells you you aren't getting enough vitamin C and this might lead to health problems later on. Which two of the following foods might you increase to reduce or eliminate the vitamin C deficiency?"

One wonders how much students might be distracted by thinking about the quirkiness of a girl who eats almost 20 pounds (19.84) of chocolate a week (the story is real).

The results from international tests have been used in scare tactics to make Americans anxious about the future. The first administration of TIMSS gave rise to a new cliché about American schools. As voiced by former secretary of education William Bennett in a speech to the Heritage Foundation, "In America today, the longer you stay in school the dumber you get relative to your peers in other industrialized nations." In this TIMSS from 1995, American fourth graders finished high among the twenty-six participating nations, eighth graders were in the middle of the pack of forty-one countries, and twelfth graders were apparently last among sixteen to nineteen countries, depending on the test.

The word *apparently* is the operative word. As noted on page 127, some American students were tested on material they hadn't studied. Many other differences among the countries made the comparisons nigh on to impossible. When I parsed the American group to find a subgroup most like their peers abroad, they finished in the middle—where they had been as eighth graders.

I do think the decline from fourth to eighth grade is likely real, for two reasons. First, for-profit publishers develop American textbooks. They want the largest market possible and so take a kitchen-sink approach. As a consequence, U.S. textbooks are about three times as thick as those in other nations. Teachers try to cover it all, leaving coverage sometimes shallow and too brief. The first TIMSS found American teachers "covering" many more topics in a year than their European or Asian peers.

Second, although we repeatedly hear algebra-in-eighth-grade calls, most of our middle school students experience the middle grades as a period of review and reinforcement. In other countries, the middle years are seen as part of the more intense study of high school.

The fear mongers invoke potential loss of economic competitiveness. As noted on pages 118–119, *A Nation at Risk* kicked off this particular bandwagon, stating we had to reform our schools in order to keep our competitive edge. Each new international study produced a new round of dire predictions about the coming economic decline. So did other studies by commissions. One headed by former senator John Glenn was titled *Before It's Too Late.* The report declared we had to reform math and science curricula before it's too late. In the report, *Before it's too late* appeared in red ink.

For an ad in the June 28, 2005, issue of the *Washington Post,* Educational Testing Service CEO Kurt Landgraf wrote, "76 percent of adults believe the U.S. will be less competitive 25 years from now if we don't fix our high schools today." Actually, the chances are this will be true no matter what we do with our high schools. Currently, the World Economic Forum ranks the United States as the most competitive nation in the world among 104 nations. A projection in the June 27 issue of the *New York Times,* though, sees China as the number one economy by 2050, with the United States second and India third (Brooke 2005). Currently, neither China nor India appears in the rankings.

In both PISA and the recent TIMSS assessments, the United States ranked in the middle of the thirty-five or so participating nations. Once again, though, the overall score masks important differences among subgroups. American students in low-poverty schools usually outscore the rest of the world while students in high-poverty schools are below average. Obviously there are affluent and poor students in other nations but (1) the United States, although the wealthiest nation in the world (discounting a few tiny anomalies like Luxembourg), has a higher proportion of students living in poverty, over 20 percent, and (2) poverty is more extreme in the United States than in other developed nations (UNICEF 2005).

From all the various international comparisons, we can induce a principle:

> **Principle of Data Interpretation:** *If a situation really is as alleged, ask, "So what?*

This principle is not an invitation to unthinking skepticism. You should then seek the "what" in "So what?" For example, if American eighth graders and tenth graders are in the middle of the pack in international comparisons, what are the ramifications and implications?

In the case of international comparisons on test scores, the situation is that American students typically score about average. This "mediocre" performance has been used to predict economic decline and a loss of global competitiveness. If we actually look into the consequences of that performance, though, there doesn't seem to have been any. As noted on page 116, the WEF ranks the United States as the most competitive nation in the world. This is because competitiveness involves so many more variables than just education. *Mediocre* was in quotes to make a point: *average* is a statistic; *mediocre* is a judgment.

Ability Versus Aptitude Versus Achievement Tests

The attempts to render conceptual differences among these three terms— *ability test, aptitude test,* and *achievement test*—has produced an enormous amount of confusion and hurt. Americans came to believe that ability tests tested potential while achievement tests tested actual skills, and aptitude tests were ability tests tailored to a more limited set of talents.

Thus, when students took ability tests followed by achievement tests and didn't do as well on the achievement tests, teachers, counselors, and parents labeled them as underachievers. In the opposite case they were called overachievers, with the implication that their effort let them outstrip their actual ability.

Because the ability test came first in time and the achievement test second, it was often also said that ability tests were used to look forward in time while achievement tests looked backward in time and summed up prior achievement. Lee Cronbach, one of the most distinguished psychometricians of the twentieth century, observed that the same test could be both an achievement test and an ability test: "The test is referred to as an achievement test when it is used to examine a person's success in past study, and as an aptitude test when it is used to forecast his success in some future course or assignment" (1960).

Any test can be used to predict anything in the future. Whether it predicts the future or not is an empirical question. We use the SAT (which used to be called a test of developed abilities, adding further fog to the confusion) to predict college grade points. We could just as well use the Iowa Tests of Educational Development, which are high school achievement tests.

The prediction is a mere statistical manipulation: We give one test at one point in time and then correlate that test with our other measure at some later point in time. We could use high school grade point average to predict college grade point average. We could use nose length to predict college grade point average. Any two variables can be correlated.

A 1982 study by the National Academy of Sciences concluded, rightly, that no test administered at one point in time measures potential. A single test can measure only what the person knows and can do at that point in time.

The real difference between an ability and an achievement test is this: An achievement test, even one that doesn't match a curriculum particularly well, has something to do with what was taught in school. The questions that turn up on an achievement test reflect to some extent what schools teach.

In contrast, we have no idea—or far less of an idea—how people learned the skills ability tests call for. The CogAT (Cognitive Abilities Test)—the ability test paired with the Iowa Tests of Basic Skills—contains a "non-verbal abilities" subtest. It requires students to mentally manipulate geometric objects. It requires people to look at a series of geometrical objects and predict which of another set should come next in the series. Some people can ace this test; some cannot handle it at all. But where did the good testers learn these skills? Not known. Incidentally, kids who score high on the nonverbal abilities and low on the other two sections of the CogAT, the quantitative and verbal sections, have a terrible time in school because school is all about words and numbers. These students are often artistic, though, or skilled at games that require perceptual skills such as video games and chess.

> **Principle of Data Interpretation:** *Achievement and ability tests differ mostly in what we know about how students learned the tested skills.*

Types of Test Formats

The Multiple-Choice Format

We are so used to seeing multiple-choice questions that we usually do not notice anything strange about them. Looked at with a neutral eye, though, the multiple-choice format is a rather peculiar way of measuring something. If the question is a four-choice multiple-choice item, the test maker must be able to trick enough people into picking the three wrong answers often enough for the item to show proper behavior. Wrong answers are typically called *distractors*.

Proper Behavior in a Test Item

As noted, proper behavior in a test item is a matter of its statistical properties, and why test publishers would want the particular properties they do is intimately bound up in the history of testing.

Historically, testing initially had only one function: to differentiate among individuals in order to make differential predictions about them in the future. The French Ministry of Education had presented psychologist Alfred Binet with a binary task: find those children who cannot benefit from regular schooling and separate them from the others. Binet did not have the multiple-choice question format for this task and could test only one child at a time. The multiple-choice format question, which permits mass and less expensive testing, was invented in 1915 by Frederick J. Kelly at the University of Kansas and quickly appropriated by Lewis Terman (who would later create the Stanford-Binet IQ test) and his colleagues working for the army in World War I. The Terman group wanted to know who would make good pilots, who would make good gunners, who was likely most capable of driving a tank, and who could do no better than be cannon fodder.

As we saw in discussing the possible correlation between height and skill at basketball, if the goal is to make discriminations among people, then different people must score differently, or predictions are impossible. It turns out that a multiple-choice test will spread people out most when most of the items are answered correctly by about 50 percent of the test takers (this figure changes a little if the test maker includes a correction for guessing). In stat talk people say an item that people get right 50 percent of the time has a p value of .50, where p stands for probability of getting the item right.

You won't find any items on norm-referenced tests that 90 percent of the norming sample got right or which only 10 percent got right. Those items were showing improper behavior, and the test developer will have tossed them out.

Another common characteristic of multiple-choice items was noticed a half century ago by one T. C. Batty, who captured it tellingly in a 1959 letter to the *Times* of London (Hoffman 1964):

Sir,
Among the "odd one out" type of questions which my son had to answer for a school entrance examination was "Which is the odd one out among cricket, football, billiards, and hockey?"

I say billiards because it is the only one played indoors. A colleague says football because it is the only one in which the ball is not struck with an implement. A neighbor says cricket because in all the other games the object is to put the ball into a net; and my son, with the confidence of nine summers, plumps for hockey "because it is the only one that is a girls' game." Could any of your readers put me out of my misery by stating what is the correct answer and further enlighten me by explaining how questions of this sort prove anything, especially when the scholar has merely to underline the odd one out without giving a reason?

Perhaps there is a remarkable subtlety behind all this. Is the question designed to test what a child of 9 may or may not know about billiards—proficiency at which may still be regarded as the sign of a misspent youth?
Yours faithfully,
T. C. Batty

The person most likely "in misery," of course, was Batty's son, who, at the ripe old age of nine, was under the gun from a high-stakes test that would limit or expand his educational horizons and his later occupational choices. *Times* readers only increased Batty's misery by sending letters that offered their own reasons for choosing one or the other among the games.

Batty had noticed a problem with most multiple-choice questions: they give no hint why students picked a particular answer. Did they guess? Had they memorized it? Did they have deep knowledge of the concept or only a surface familiarity that let them pick the right answer but not use the concept? Did they reason their way to a right answer? Did they reason their way to a *wrong*—officially wrong, anyway—answer?

Young children are particularly apt to have good reasons for choosing wrong answers. For example, in one locale young children were asked, "What animal is most likely to be found on a farm? Elephant, giraffe, chicken, fox?" Most children picked giraffe. A nearby petting zoo named Animal Farm used a wooden giraffe to mark its entrance.

Some multiple-choice questions can give you some diagnostic information about what is going on in the child's head, but not many. Most of them are found on math tests, where the answers might indicate that this child is having trouble with place value or that one has difficulty converting a fraction to a decimal, for example.

Short-Answer Questions

It has long been held by psychologists that it requires a deeper understanding to *produce* an answer on a test than to simply *select* an answer, as one does with multiple-choice questions. Short-answer questions are popular because they are short: while not as many can be used in the same amount of time as multiple-choice questions, enough can be used to sample a wide range of knowledge. Similarly, short-answer questions cannot be scored at the nanospeeds that are available to multiple-choice answer sheets, but they can be handled quickly—and many essays cannot. Essays are intended to evoke thinking and contemplation in students and the students' responses often evoke thinking and contemplation in teachers. Short-answer questions also save the test constructor the sometimes arduous task of finding three distractors for a multiple-choice item that students will find credible.

Essay Questions and Portfolios

Because of the writing samples in mass-administered state examinations, we now know how many sentences constitute an essay. Five. An essay consists of an opening topic sentence, three supporting sentences, and a closing sentence. This is what children are learning from taking writing tests in a number of states. Scoring writing samples that actually reflected real writing would be time-consuming and highly expensive. Most companies that specialize in scoring state-administered writing samples employ temps at seven or eight dollars an hour. They might spend as little as fifteen seconds grading an "essay." Students who creatively drift from the 1-3-1 formula above might well suffer penalties.

The traditional grousing says essays are unreliable, are scored in part on the basis of handwriting and, especially, length. Still, if the goal of the examination is to see how well students have attained complex educational outcomes and how well they can put ideas together, there is nothing to top a good essay question.

The new SAT writing test gives students twenty-five minutes to write. At least two people read the essay with a third brought in if the first two have judged it quite differently. That, of course, is the major source of the alleged unreliability of essay questions: they are unreliable because different people judge them differently. And at times, judges do differ because they bring different criteria to the judging act. Some people, including me, object to on-demand writing samples because we feel that editing and revision are integral parts of the process. Red Smith, a sportswriter good enough to be called simply a writer, explained the essence of the process: "You just sit down at the typewriter and open a vein."

The rap on the new SAT essay question is that length counts for everything and errors for nothing. The official scorer's guide says, "You are scoring the writing not the correctness of facts" (Winerip 2005a, B9). Doesn't sound like a wholly sound approach to me. The College Board might be of like mind: it hedges its bet on the writing test by including forty-nine multiple-choice items that count for 75 percent of the score.

Teachers usually look to score both the writing *and* the content. This sometimes frustrates students. I have spent more than a few hours trying to convince a student that his answer to a question received a lower grade than another person's similar answer to the same question because the clarity and style of writing counted. I'd say that they didn't go to hear so-and-so in concert just because they played the right notes or sang in tune. Style counts.

It used to be, maybe still is, common to say that multiple-choice questions are hard to write but easy to score while writing essay questions is easy, but scoring them is hard. It's hard to create a question that unambiguously directs the student to one and only one right answer (assuming for the moment that multiple answers such as "A and C above" are not on the test) but has properly behaving distractors. You can write a good essay question, though, and not know what the right answer is. Many professors would write such questions and then sample the answers to induce what looked like a good response. When I taught at universities, I used this technique to some extent. I would write down the rough outlines of a scoring guide, but I could never anticipate the creativity that some students would show or the lines of argumentation they would follow. Sampling the answers was necessary to frame a notion of the full range of answers.

A portfolio is a collection of "essays," in quotes because it might also contain fiction and poetry or even a script. Portfolios have the great advantage over on-demand essays of incorporating editing and revision. At least, those of us who revise and edit a lot in our own writing think that is a great advantage.

Portfolios are not without problems, though. One is, what goes in? Typical work or the best work? Who decides what is best? Teacher or student? They often have different opinions. As do, actually, multiple teachers. The failure of teachers to agree on a grade for a portfolio has been cited by psychometricians as evidence of unreliability. I think it is evidence of the limitations of the psychometric concept of reliability (presented on page 145). Judging a portfolio is a complex process and it should not surprise us that different teachers bring different perspectives to the task any more than it would surprise us that different movie critics often differ violently on the merits of a film. Nevertheless, portfolios have been largely abandoned as parts of a formal assessment program.

Prince George's County: A Cautionary Tale

In the 1980s, one John Murphy arrived as the new superintendent in Prince George's County, Maryland. Like many new superintendents, Murphy announced a series of goals and promises. Murphy promised to get test scores up generally and close the black-white achievement gap (PG, as it's known, is a large suburban district bordering on the District of Columbia and at the time of Murphy's arrival was about two-thirds African American and one-third white).

On the walls of a conference room next to his office, Murphy posted charts showing test score trends in each school. Murphy dubbed this his "applied anxiety room." In the ensuing years, test scores rose. The black-white gap, while it did not close, shrank substantially, and black students' scores escalated comfortably above the national norm. But rumors were heard that in some schools, instruction looked suspiciously like test preparation: students would go to the blackboard, read a short statement, and choose one of a set of answers to a question.

Several organizations proposed external evaluations. Murphy resisted.

Maryland had used a particular test as its state test far too long for the test to remain viable as an accurate assessment. After a test's repeated use, teachers are used to the questions and may shift instruction; curriculum changes make some questions obsolete, and so on. In addition, a number of psychometricians thought that the norms for this particular edition of the test, the 1972 CTBS, were too low, meaning they thought it was too easy to score well.

Finally, Maryland changed tests. Test scores fell across the state, a common phenomenon when a new test is adopted. But in PG, they plummeted.

The ethnic gap yawned as large as ever. Scores for African American students fell as low as the eighteenth percentile.

Fortunately for Murphy, he had already landed a job in another state.

> **Principle of Data Interpretation:** *Rising test scores do not necessarily mean rising achievement.*

Rising test scores might be the same as rising achievement if the test could cover everything that the students learned, but most tests are twenty-five to forty items long and can't possibly cover such a range. When the focus is on the test, other parts of the curriculum are deemphasized or ignored altogether.

Even among psychometricians, the validity of testing rests on an assumption: The items on the test are a representative sample of the domain being tested, for example, mathematics. The student is presumed to be able to transfer his knowledge displayed on the test items to the rest of the domain. To concentrate on just what the test covers—to teach to the test—renders that assumption false and destroys the usefulness of the test. The students in Prince George's could not transfer their knowledge to another part of the domain of mathematics; their knowledge was limited to the domain covered by the old test.

In the realm of testing, this outcome is known as the law of WYTIWYG, pronounced witty-wig.

> **Principle of Data Interpretation:** *The law of WYTIWYG applies: What you test is what you get.*

So you need to exercise some care in what you test for.

Two Essential Qualities of Tests: Reliability and Validity

The absolutely essential quality of a test is its validity. But there is a prior characteristic that must be demonstrated: reliability. A reliable test might not be valid, but an unreliable test cannot be valid.

Reliability

Reliability in a test is a measure of stability. Do people who score high or low one time tend to score the same way a second time? Actually, these days, test developers seldom give the same test twice to obtain what is called a test-retest reliability estimate. The amount of time between the first and second tests is problematic—too brief and people remember how they answered the first time; too long and intervening learning can shift the scores meaningfully but in a way that lowers the statistic used to calculate reliability. A test-retest reliability measure also slows down the development process and adds to the costs.

Today, reliability is estimated from a single administration of the test by correlating the results from half the items with the results from the other half and so is called a split-half reliability. We could correlate the odd-numbered items with the even-numbered or the first half of the items with the second half. The latter is not such a good idea as fatigue might affect the second half, or the last half of the items might be systematically different from the first half (for many tests, items get increasingly difficult as you progress through the questions). In fact, mathematically, the statistics that are used to estimate reliability represent the average of all possible split-half reliabilities. A reliability coefficient is a particular instance of a correlation coefficient (for the record, the two reliability coefficients you are most likely to encounter are called the Kuder-Richardson formula 20, or KR-20, and the Cronbach Alpha). In order to provide an adequate index of stability, a reliability coefficient should exceed +.80, and the closer it gets to +1.0, the better. Most commercial tests have reliabilities in the area of +.90.

Validity

I consider here the four types of validity with the most practical importance to practicing educators: content, predictive or criterion, curriculum, and instructional. I also give some attention to two additional important theoretical conceptions of validity, construct validity and consequential validity.

Content validity is arrived at by judgments of content experts, who decide if the test truly measures what it claims to measure.

Predictive or *criterion validity* refers to how well we can use the test at one time to predict some other event at a later time. We've talked a lot on these pages about the predictive validity of the SAT, used to predict freshman college grade point averages. Because there is a correlation between SAT scores and that grade point, we can accurately infer that the SAT can be used to predict grades, although by no means perfectly.

Curriculum validity asks whether or not the test covers material actually in the curriculum while *instructional validity* goes one step further and asks if the students were actually taught the material. These concepts emerged from the *Debra P. v. Turlington* case mentioned on page 125. The judges in the case argued that the state could use passing the test as a prerequisite for a high school diploma only after it had demonstrated instructional validity. One could not accurately infer that students had failed to learn the skills called for without evidence that they had actually had the opportunity to learn them. The judges used the phrase *curriculum validity,* but by reading their brief it becomes obvious that instructional validity is what they had in mind.

Two other types of validity, construct and consequential, need to be mentioned.

In *Modern Educational Measurement,* testing guru James Popham begs his readers to read the section on construct validity slowly because "the ideas presented therein are apt to be foreign to your experience. Indeed, they are apt to be foreign to anyone's experience" (2000, 105). Construct validity doesn't pop up much in the daily lives of practicing educators, but it's an important notion and I borrow from Popham's discussion.

Popham first imagines a person who envisions a hypothetical construct he calls "love of animals." Then that person develops the Animal Lover's Inventory (ALI) to measure the construct. He administers the ALI to people entering the City Dog Pound with an animal and to those leaving the pound with an animal. The person hypothesizes that people leaving with an animal will score higher than people arriving with an animal because people taking an animal away from the shelter are saving an animal from being put down. If the people leaving with animals do in fact score higher on the ALI than those arriving, then we would say that the experiment provided construct-related validity evidence for the existence of the construct "love of animals."

Constructs for which people have developed tests and inventories include intelligence, anxiety, self-esteem, and introversion.

In the late 1980s Samuel Messick, a psychometrician at Educational Testing Service, brought forth the argument that the *consequences* of a test were part of a test's validity and people began to speak of consequential validity. Suppose once a test is introduced to a state teachers start to spend more time teaching material the test covers. Schools retain in grade students who score low on the test. Or students near the cut score receive extra instruction to help get them over the threshold. Those are consequences of the test use. Messick considered such consequences as part of a test's validity. (I picked three consequences well documented as a result of high-stakes testing.)

Not all psychometricians agree. No one denies that tests have consequences, certainly. The debate centers on whether those consequences should be considered an aspect of *validity.* Note that in the previous examples of various validities, I often used the phrase *accurately infer.* For a number of testing professionals, validity should refer to the *accuracy of inferences made from test results* and nothing more.

Popham, for instance, imagines the creation of a test that everyone agrees is a great test of mathematics. He then has a school board declare that girls who score low on the test be prohibited from taking art or music courses and that boys who score low be expelled. These are consequences, clearly, but the onset of stupid policies has no bearing on the accuracy of the inferences made from the test results about whether students did or did know mathematics. They should not be considered a part of validity.

Similarly, many consequences flow from the tests administered because of the No Child Left Behind law. Most of these tests, maybe all, have passed the test for content validity. If the data from these tests result in the takeover of public schools by private educational management organizations—one possible consequence built into the law—should that consequence be considered part of the test's validity? Many would argue no.

> **Principle of Data Interpretation:** *Any tests offered by a publisher should present adequate evidence of both reliability and validity.*

A Few Specific Tests

The National Assessment of Educational Progress

"Yes, the problem with NAEP is keeping the students awake during the test." Thus spoke Archie Lapointe, then the executive director of NAEP, in response to my comment that NAEP systematically underestimated achievement because students, especially seventeen-year-old students, didn't take it seriously. NAEP provides no feedback to students, teachers, parents, or school and district administrators. Although there has been a try-out of NAEP with a few large cities, the smallest unit that NAEP currently reports is the state.

NAEP is taken more seriously now than it was when I made the comment some ten years ago and it might soon come to be taken *too* seriously. More about that anon.

Commissioner of Education Francis Keppel brought NAEP into existence in the late 1960s through the efforts of polymath Ralph Tyler.[2] Keppel wanted something that would do for education what health statistics did for medicine. For instance, to know how serious the nation's problem with tuberculosis was, and therefore how much effort would be needed to eradicate it, you needed to have some data about its incidence. Keppel wanted NAEP to describe what people knew and what they didn't know. Once we knew that, we could debate about whether or not most people knew what they needed to know or whether schools needed improving.

To accomplish this end, NAEP asked questions that were typical of NRTs—questions that about half the respondents got right. But it also asked questions that its developers expected almost everyone to know and questions they expected very few people to know. They envisioned NAEP as a purely descriptive assessment.

When Keppel proposed NAEP, virtually every education organization in the country rose up in opposition. They saw it as eventually leading to a national curriculum and federal control of education. To get NAEP approved and funded by Congress, Keppel had to agree to not report results below the regional level (e.g., the Northeast) and to house the operation not in his offices but at the Education Commission of the States, a state-level policy organization, where it would be safe from federal meddling.

NAEP proved to be a lucrative contract and some companies began to object to ECS receiving the contract in a sole-source, noncompetitive award. In 1982, the U.S. Department of Education agreed to competitive bids for NAEP and the competition was won by Educational Testing Service. ETS launched a drive to make NAEP more visible by calling it the Nation's Report Card. NAEP came to test reading and mathematics every two years, science every four, and other subjects—writing, civics, history, geography, and art—less often.

---

2. Commissioner, not secretary, because at the time the Office of Education was part of the Department of Health, Education, and Welfare, not a separate cabinet-level department as it is today.

In 1988 Congress amended the law governing NAEP to permit state-level comparisons. At the same time, it brought the National Assessment Governing Board into existence to determine NAEP policy. The NAGB's first president, former assistant secretary of education Chester Finn, was charged with establishing achievement levels for NAEP. This fundamentally changed NAEP. Keppel had wanted a purely *descriptive* assessment about what people do and don't know. Finn wanted a *prescriptive* assessment about what people *ought* to know.

The achievement levels—basic, proficient, and advanced—were set ludicrously high and led to demeaning statements about the competence of students and, by implication, the competence of teachers and the quality of schools. NAEP's executive director, Lapointe, once said that "only $7\frac{1}{2}$ percent of our three million high school seniors" leave high school with "an ability to integrate scientific information with other knowledge." Albert Shanker, president of the American Federation of Teachers, pointed out that the assessment of seniors was an assessment of successful students, the dropouts having left, but "the findings of the NAEP indicate that few of these students are ready to do real college-level work or to handle a good job."

The use of the achievement levels sustained and perhaps even augmented the sense of crisis created by 1983's *A Nation at Risk.*

The problem with the achievement levels, though, is that they are no damn good. The Government Accounting Office, the Center for Research on Evaluation, Standards, and Student Testing, the National Academy of Sciences, and the National Academy of Education have all weighed in on the achievement levels and they have all said, politely of course, these levels are no damn good.

Even the NAEP reports themselves issue a disclaimer citing the various studies mentioned in the preceding paragraph. Here's a quote from the National Academy of Sciences that appears in the NAEP reports: "NAEP's current achievement level setting procedures remain fundamentally flawed. The judgment tasks are difficult and confusing; raters' judgments of different item types are internally inconsistent; appropriate validity evidence for the cut scores is lacking and the procedures have produced unreasonable results."

Fundamentally flawed? Unreasonable results? Missing validity evidence? Can you imagine the scorn that would be heaped upon ETS or CTB/McGraw-Hill if it dared bring to market a product with these deficiencies? The report goes on to say the levels should be interpreted with caution (they aren't) and only until something better is constructed. No one is working on making better standards largely because there is so much political mileage in pointing to apparently low achievement and saying we have to get tough with the schools. Many governors, state legislators, and state and local school board members have made getting tough with schools a major plank in their platforms.

In fairness, it must be said that NAEP poses unusual challenges to someone who would create meaningful achievement levels, primarily because no student "takes a NAEP" in the same way that kids take an SAT or an ITBS. NAEP wishes to assess a wide range of knowledge and skills. A total NAEP assessment is extremely long, and no individual student answers more than a third of the questions. NAEP uses a procedure called matrix sampling to obtain reliable estimates of what proportion of students answer each item correctly. For a test such as the ACT we can say how a student's ACT achievement level will serve him in the future. We can say a student with an ACT math score of X has Y chance of passing, say, college algebra. We can say that because each student takes the entire ACT and has an individual score. The ACT developers in Iowa City have conducted empirical studies to determine how students with different scores fare with their college courses. No such statements can be made for NAEP because there is no score attached to an individual.

Still, here's an example of what the National Academy of Sciences had in mind when it said the levels produce unreasonable results: The 1996 NAEP science assessment declared that only 29 percent of fourth graders were proficient or better. But the TIMSS fourth-grade science assessment, administered in the same year, found American fourth graders third in the world among twenty-fix mostly developed nations. An earlier NAEP said only 32 percent of American fourth graders could read proficiently, but an international assessment the same year found only Finnish children reading better. The fourth graders in twenty-five other countries finished behind the American students in the study. The results produced from the achievement levels are indeed "unreasonable."

But here's the danger. It lies in that word *proficient.* Proficient is what 100 percent of American students must be by the year 2014, according to No Child Left Behind. Currently each state uniquely defines proficient under NCLB. This bothers some because such unique definitions permit no state-by-state comparisons. But, ah, if we used NAEP . . . and it just so happens that NCLB changed state-level NAEP from voluntary to mandatory. Paul Peterson at Harvard, Frederick Hess at the American Enterprise Institute, Diane

Ravitch of New York University, and Chester Finn, now at the Thomas B. Fordham Foundation, have all proposed using NAEP as the common yardstick.

That would be a disaster. But for those who are ever vigilant for reasons to privatize the public schools, it would be an opportunity.

There are actually two NAEPs: the regular NAEP and the NAEP for trends. For trend analysis, NAEP has used the same set of items since the 1970s. Most scores have been trending up, and the attempt of Secretary of Education Margaret Spellings to attribute the most recent gains seen in the 2004 trends to NCLB was unseemly and wrong. The last previous trend data had been collected in 1999. Thus, three years had elapsed before NCLB came into existence, and the first year of that existence might be termed No Educator Left Unconfused—it is doubtful that any progress was made in the 2002–3 school year.

The regular NAEP generates the reports that ETS and the Department of Education label the Nation's Report Card. While these assessments contain many items from previous assessments, they add or remove items to keep in step with curricular trends. For instance, the NAEP math assessment contains items more in line with the National Council of Teachers of Mathematics' curriculum standards promulgated in 1989. This bothers some observers, who contend that the NCTM standards do not give adequate weight to traditional mathematics skills such as computation.

The SAT

We have already discussed the SAT in terms of its power to predict freshman college grades (page 78) and in terms of its twenty years of falling scores from 1963 to 1982 (page 118). A little history here.

The SAT, née the Scholastic Aptitude Test, was brought into existence in 1926 by the College Entrance Examination Board, an organization then serving mostly institutions of higher education in the Northeast. The board had been giving essay tests to prospective college attendees since it was formed in 1900. The board had been much impressed by the work of Terman and his colleagues with multiple-choice questions during World War I and the first SAT was a mix of multiple-choice items and essays. The essay section was abandoned entirely after the U.S. entrance into World War II in 1941 interfered with its administration schedule.

The SAT was first referred to as an IQ test and later as a test of "developed abilities," an elegantly vague term. As both, though, it was seen as an addition to the high school record, not as a replacement for it. The 1926 words of its principal developer, Carl Campbell Brigham, cannot be improved on:

> The present state of all efforts of men to measure or in any way estimate the worth of other men, or to evaluate the results of their nurture or to reckon their potential possibilities does not warrant any certainty of prediction. . . . This additional test now made available through the instrumentality of the College Entrance Examination Board may help to resolve a few perplexing problems, but it should be regarded merely as a supplementary record. To place too great emphasis on test scores is as dangerous as the failure to properly evaluate any score or rank in conjunction with other measures and estimates which it supplements. (44–45)

The SAT was to be a supplement to the rest of the high school data, one piece of data, nothing more.

The 1941 administration of the SAT served as its standard-setting administration. For that, 10,654 students took the test. Ninety-eight percent were white, 61 percent were male, and 41 percent had attended private, college-preparatory high schools. An elite, in other words. It was this elite for which a mean of 500 was assigned as the average standard score (see pages 159–162 for a discussion of standard scores). By 1995, the test-taking sample looked very different. In that year, 1,067,993 seniors, about 42 percent of the nation's senior class, sat for the SAT. Sixty-nine percent of those huddled in angst on Saturday mornings were white, 46 percent were male, and only 17 percent had attended private schools of any kind. Twenty-three percent reported family incomes of less than thirty thousand dollars.

The impact of these demographic changes on SAT score interpretation bothered the board. If a student scored 470 on the SAT verbal, she would consider herself below average. And she would be—but only in reference to the standard-setting elite of 1941 to which all later scores were referenced. Her status vis-à-vis her million-odd peers taking the SAT was unknown.

The board decided to recenter—that is, renorm—the SAT. The recentering made a score of 500 representative of the average person applying to a four-year college. It made eminently good sense to me. Conservative school critics howled and accused the board of trying to hide ignorance. Chester Finn called the recentering "the largest dose of educational Prozac in the history of the nation."

Actually, the recentering affected mostly the verbal score. For the math it made little difference. In fact, the number of correct answers that generate scores in the range between 660 and 710 on the recentered scale generate higher standard scores on the old scale. That is, the new scale is tougher, not easier. A student whose raw score received a 690 on the old scale would receive only a 680 on the recentered scale.

IQ Tests

IQ tests entered the education arena early in the twentieth century when the French Ministry of Education assigned clinical psychologist Alfred Binet the task of developing a test that would identify those students who could not benefit from a regular French school regime. Binet, a compassionate man, worried a great deal over his task, knowing that such identification would have an enormous social and economic impact on the students so identified.

Binet wasn't even sure what was important to test. He set up a couple of criteria for a test to be included. First, older students must perform better than younger students. Second, Binet assigned a "mental age" to a test. A test had a mental age of six if 80 percent of six-year-olds got it right. Each test was worth a mental age of six months. All this is thoughtful but, of course, rather arbitrary—Binet had no precedents to give him guidance.

Binet assigned children mental ages depending on how many tests they completed. A German psychologist, Wilhelm Stern, pointed out that knowing only a person's mental age could mislead: a person who was chronologically five years old and had a mental age of eight was quite different, mentally, from someone who was twelve years old and had a mental age of eight.

Stern suggested dividing the mental age by the chronological age and calling the resulting quotient the intelligence quotient, or IQ. In the previous example, the five-year-old has an IQ of 1.6 while the twelve-year-old has an IQ of .67. Stern also suggested multiplying the IQ by 100 to get rid of the decimals, in the example leaving IQs of 160 and 67, respectively.

$$IQ = \frac{MA}{CA} \times 100$$

This calculation of IQ wasn't wholly satisfactory. A person who was five and had a mental age of eight had an IQ of 160. A person who was ten and had a mental age of thirteen had an IQ of 130. Yet both people had mental ages three years ahead of average. The result has been the use of the "deviation IQ." When an IQ test is constructed or renormed, the average IQ is by fiat set to 100 using standard scores (see page 159).

This still isn't 100 percent satisfactory because it forces the average IQ to be 100. That gives the IQ an apparent stability that is not there. When New Zealand researcher James Flynn calculated cross-generational effects for Americans, he found that we had been getting smarter. The Flynn effect, as it is called, was greeted with some skepticism initially but has been replicated in numerous other nations. No one is quite sure why IQs have risen. Smaller families, better nutrition, increased education, and earlier maturation have all been put forward as possibilities.

Binet worked with a concept he called *intelligence in general.* If Binet had six tests, a person who got tests 1, 2, 3, 4, and 5 correct but failed 6 would be the same to Binet as someone who got 1 and 2 correct, failed 3, and then successfully completed 4, 5, and 6. In general, both people are the same.

When Binet's ideas crossed the Atlantic to America, though, the concept of intelligence in general changed in a subtle but profound way to *general intelligence.* Many American psychologists operated with three principles:

1. Intelligence influences every aspect of life.

2. Intelligence is a unitary entity controlled by a single gene.

3. IQ tests measure intelligence.

The leading proponent of this view, H. H. Goddard, once told an audience of Princeton freshmen:

> Now the fact is, that workmen may have a ten-year intelligence (the intelligence of a 10-year-old) while you have a 20. To demand for him such a home as you enjoy is as absurd as it would be to insist that every laborer should receive a graduate fellowship. How can there be such a thing as social equality with this wide range of mental capacity? (Gould 1981, 160)

Obviously, Goddard thought Americans had already been pretty well sorted out by intelligence and this was as it should be. Elsewhere he said, "Democracy means that the people rule by selecting the wisest most intelligent to tell them what to do to be happy. Thus Democracy is a method for arriving at a truly benevolent aristocracy" (Gould 1981, 160).

Such nonsense would have been laughable had Goddard and others working with IQ not had such a profound impact for a time on American education and social policy. Goddard tested the IQs of immigrants arriving at Ellis Island and concluded that between 67 percent and 80 percent (depending on ethnicity) were retarded. He didn't fuss over whether his translations were accurate or the fact that many immigrants had never held a pencil until Goddard thrust one into their hands.

Goddard's measurements of immigrants occurred at a time when many of them were arriving from southern and eastern Europe. His work influenced Congress to role back immigration quotas in 1924 to 1890 levels, levels much more favorable to northern Europeans. President Coolidge signed the bill, saying, "America must be kept American" (Gould 1981).

To be sure, there were some psychologists who argued that there were many different, independent abilities that went into intelligence. Most noteworthy among these were E. E. Thurstone and his concept of primary mental abilities, and J. P. Guilford, whose structure of intellect theory featured 120 independent components. The contentions for separate, independent intelligences takes its modern form in Howard Gardner's theory of multiple intelligences, as described in his 1983 book, *Frames of Mind.* Gardner therein postulates seven intelligences and lays out criteria for identifying an intelligence. He has subsequently added two to the list.

Types of Test Scores

Grade Equivalents, or GEs

We first met grade equivalents and noted the mischief they can cause in the pop quiz on pages 109–110. There we learned that the grade level of a test is the score of the median student in that grade, and, therefore, half of all students are always below grade level. We also learned that a fourth grader whose test report says she is reading at the seventh-grade level has the same score as the average seventh grader reading fourth-grade material.

The fact that using grade levels puts half of the students below grade level sometimes gets overlooked in judging schools. Many a journalist and legislator has harrumphed that in X district only 70 percent of the graduating class was reading at the twelfth-grade level. The harrumphs are particularly loud and indignant if the district in question is one of some affluence.

But, of course, the district is performing above average, since in a district representative of the nation at large, 50 percent of the graduating class would not be reading at grade level.

Mischief also occurs when people average grade levels. The violence done to accuracy is probably not great, but it is a mistake, as explained in the box on scales. Averaging grade equivalents is a bit like averaging addresses. The meaningfulness of the result is in doubt.

Scale: A System of Ordered Marks at Fixed Intervals

This is how my dictionary defines *scale:* "a system of ordered marks at fixed intervals." For scientists, the situation is a little more subtle. Scientists speak of nominal, ordinal, equal interval, and equal ratio scales.

A *nominal scale* is hardly a scale at all. The numbers have no systematic relationship to anything. The jerseys of a basketball team might be said to form a nominal scale. The numbers are unrelated to height or position or ability.

In an *ordinal scale* increasing numbers mean an increasing quantity of something, but it's not clear by how much. As noted, house addresses are an ordinal scale. So are grade equivalents. A grade equivalent of 5.0 is one grade bigger than a grade equivalent of 4.0, but we don't know what that means in terms of skills, knowledge, or behavior. If we did, we'd be well on our way to developing a true CRT. Because we don't have knowledge of how much larger one GE is from another in terms of behavior, it is not feasible to average grade equivalents.

An *equal interval scale* does embody the definition of *scale* in the first sentence of this section. Each interval is equal to every other interval in something. The temperature scales on thermometers are equal interval scales. Each degree represents the same amount of heat. Few scales in education attain this vaunted status. But even the equal interval scale has a shortcoming: you can't compare quantities in terms of "twice as much" or "half as much" or any other proportion.

For instance, we can't say that 30 degrees Celsius is twice as much heat as 15 degrees Celsius. You can see this immediately by transposing from Celsius to the Fahrenheit scale. The numbers become 86 degrees and 59 degrees, respectively. Thus we can't talk in terms of proportions—that X is twice as much as Y or A is half the size of B. The equal interval scales lack a 0 that's really 0. It is true that 0 degrees Celsius has a meaning: it's the point where water freezes. But that happens at 32 degrees Fahrenheit. Both 0 and 32 represent the same amount of heat. We could turn temperature into a ratio scale if we went to the Kelvin scale. Zero on the Kelvin scale is where all molecular motion stops, −273 degrees Fahrenheit.

Length is an *equal ratio scale.* Zero length is zero—can't get shorter. Now we really can talk about ratios. Two feet is twice as long as one foot.

The description of scales leads to a principle:

Principle of Data Interpretation: *Make certain that descriptions of data do not include improper statements about the type of scale being used, for example, "The gain in math is twice as large as the gain in reading."*

Percentile Ranks

As I have already said, a percentile rank is not a score. It's, well, it's a rank. Percentiles don't form an equal interval scale. The distance between the fiftieth and sixtieth percentiles is much smaller than the distance between the eightieth and ninetieth percentiles. This can be seen by looking at Figure 6 (on page 49), which shows a normal curve and how the various scales fit on it.

Normal Curve Equivalents

Normal curve equivalents, or NCEs, were supposed to create an equal interval scale for test results. As you can see from Figure 6, they *are* arrayed at equal intervals along the normal curve. But they don't have a meaningful psychological component. That is, we really have no theoretical basis for saying that the amount of learning represented by a move from 30 to 40 NCEs is the same as that represented by a move from 40 to 50.

NCEs are not used much anymore because, unlike percentile ranks or grade equivalents, they have no intuitive meaning. You know that if a child scores at the sixtieth percentile on a test, he scored better than 60 percent of the people in the national norming sample, and if he scores at the seventieth percentile on the next test, he overtook another 10 percent of the people in the national norming sample.

If your child scores an NCE of 60 on a test, it means . . . what? You'd have to look it up, and you'd see that she scored better than 78 percent of the norming sample. And if she moves up to 70, you'd have to look it up again and find out that she scored better than 83 percent of the norming sample. Too clunky.

Stanines

I was surprised recently to receive some test results reported in stanines. I thought that these days they were used only to hide bad news or to make a school or district look better to the press.

Stanine is short for "standard nine," and stanines are a compression of percents. They come from the era when we used the "do not fold, spindle, or mutilate" punch cards to enter information into computers. Those cards held just eighty columns for information, so each column was precious. Many test scores used as many as three digits or three columns. Someone in the Air Force realized that for most test results, if you could collapse the numbers into a single digit, you would save two of these precious columns. Each stanine represents some part of the normal curve, distributed as follows:

Stanine	1	2	3	4	5	6	7	8	9
Percent of Normal Curve	4	7	12	17	20	17	12	7	4

It became common practice to consider stanines 4, 5, and 6 as average. Stanines 1, 2, and 3 are below average, 7, 8, and 9, above average. Let's assume your school district has the exact same achievement as the national norming sample: your average percentile rank would then be 50, and 50 percent of your students would be above average and 50 percent would be below average.

But you can make achievement seem higher by shifting to stanines. The three middle stanines, 4, 5, and 6, contain 54 percent of all scores. Stanines 7, 8, and 9 contain another 23 percent, and are usually labeled "above average." So, you can tell your public or the media that 77 percent of all students scored average or above average. Only the 23 percent of the scores in the bottom three stanines have to be reported as "below average." It ain't Lake Wobegon, but it's getting close.

Standard or Scaled Scores

Standard scores are the most technical of the test scores and the most widely used as well. You no doubt play with them all the time, but might not be aware of what you're handling. An IQ is a standard score. So are the scores on the SAT, ACT, NAEP, GRE, LSAT, GMAT, TIMSS, PISA, and so forth. Most of the commercial norm-referenced tests are reported in something other than standard scores, but they could be so reported: they come with something that will be called a growth scale or a developmental scale, and these, too, are standard scores. Sometimes they are called z scores, which is just a naming convention, and sometimes, just to confuse things, they are called scaled scores. All scores occur on some kind of scale, but if you're reading something that talks about scaled scores, it is talking about standard scores.

People in schools seldom use standard scores, which is too bad because that probably means that some kids get the wrong grade on their report card. Before we address this problem, though, we need to know where standard scores come from.

We make standard scores by converting raw scores into scores in terms of how big they are in standard deviation units. This will all become clear momentarily.

Imagine a set of test scores where the mean is 50 and the standard deviation is 10. Suppose this set of scores contains scores of 20, 30, 40, 50, 60, 70, and 80 (for convenience, I am using only scores that will generate standard scores that are whole numbers).

Suppose we take each raw score, subtract the mean from it, and divide by the standard deviation:

$$(20 - 50) \div 10 = -3 \qquad (60 - 50) \div 10 = +1$$

$$(30 - 50) \div 10 = -2 \qquad (70 - 50) \div 10 = +2$$

$$(40 - 50) \div 10 = -1 \qquad (80 - 50) \div 10 = +3$$

$$(50 - 50) \div 10 = 0$$

Notice anything about the relationship of the raw scores to the corresponding standard scores?

Take 80 as an example. If the mean is 50 and the standard deviation is 10, then a score of 80 is three standard deviations above the mean. It yields a standard score of +3.0. A score of 70 is two standard deviations above the mean and, miracle of miracles, it yields a standard score of +2.0.

Converting to standard scores as we just did always yields a score in terms of how far above or below the mean it is in standard deviation units. In our example, a score of 30 is two standard deviations below the mean of 50 and thus yields a standard score of −2.

Suppose now we give a test and Mary gets a 70 percent correct on it; then on a second test she gets a 73 percent. If we're grading just on the absolute percentage correct, then she did better on the second test. But it might seem fairer to grade her on the tests in terms of how well she did relative to the other students.

Let's assume that the average on the first test was 60 percent correct and on the second, 65 percent correct. Mary thus scored ten points above average on the first test, but only eight points above the average on the second. But let us further suppose that the standard deviation was 5 on the first test and 10 on the second.

On the first test Mary scored a full two standard deviations above the mean ($[70 - 60] \div 5 = 2$) whereas she scored only .8 standard deviations above the mean ($[73 - 65] \div 10 = .8$) on the second. Mary gave us an above-average performance on both tests, but it was more above on the first test. A +2.0 standard deviations puts her above 98 percent of the people taking the first test (she would be above the 50 percent of the test takers below average and above the 34 percent between the mean and +1 standard deviations and the 14 percent that are between +1 and +2 standard deviations, a total of 98 percent of all people). The results are shown in Figure 31. As a reminder, these figures are strictly true only for normal, bell-shaped curves, not skewed distributions.

Her score on the second test puts her above 79 percent of the people. I know this because I just looked it up in a statistics book.

Now you may be perplexed because I've shown the standard scores running from −3 to +3 and they don't look anything like the SAT that goes from 200 to 800 or an IQ test that would run from 55 to 145. But it's easy to get from where we are, −3 to +3, to either of these other oft-used scales.

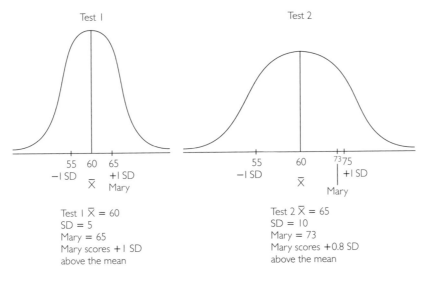

FIG. 31   Mary's Performance on Two Tests

Watch closely. I take each standard score, multiply by fifteen, and add one hundred:

$$-3 \times 15 + 100 = 55$$

$$-2 \times 15 + 100 = 70$$

$$-1 \times 15 + 100 = 85$$

$$0 \times 15 + 100 = 100$$

$$+1 \times 15 + 100 = 115$$

$$+2 \times 15 + 100 = 130$$

$$+3 \times 15 + 100 = 145$$

Voilà! In the right-hand column, the distribution of IQ: a mean of 100 and a standard deviation of 15.

If I had multiplied by one hundred and added five hundred, I've have gotten the SAT scale, where the mean is 500 and the standard deviation is 100. You might want to try that just to see that it works.

We make this kind of transformation for two reasons. First, the human brain does not like decimals. It much prefers whole numbers. Second, we use different scales for different tests in order to minimize confusion. No one will confuse an IQ scale with its mean of 100 and standard deviation of 15 with an SAT scale where the mean is 500 and the standard deviation 100. The ACT battery and NAEP use different scales still.

The important point: Multiplying the standard score by a constant (fifteen in this case) and then adding a constant (one hundred in this case) does not alter the relationship among the scores. In stat speak, you have made a "linear transformation" of the scores, leaving their relationship unchanged. If we had squared any numbers or taken the square root, or raised them to a higher exponent, we'd have made nonlinear transformations and the relationships would have changed.

Abuses of Testing

> The more any quantitative social indicator is used for social decision-making, the more subject it will be to corruption pressures and the more apt it will be to distort and corrupt the social processes it is intended to monitor. (Campbell 1975)

Over the years a number of common abuses of testing have emerged. Among the most common are the use of a test for a purpose other than what it was designed for and the use of a single test to make important decisions about individuals or groups. The *Standards for Educational and Psychological Testing* promulgated jointly by the American Educational Research Association, the National Council on Measurement in Education, and the American Psychological Association condemn both types of abuses. These abuses have even been condemned by commercial test publishers, although no publisher has ever refused to sell its tests to an acknowledged abuser. You might want to look at the American Educational Research Association's position statement on high-stakes testing derived from the *Standards,* at www.aera.net/policyandprograms/?id=378.

As an example of using a test for a different purpose, consider the proper use of a norm-referenced test. These tests are designed to measure the performance of people against the performance of other people. They are not designed to evaluate students on an absolute scale or to evaluate a teacher at all. Indeed, they are designed to be *insensitive* to instruction.

> **Principle of Data Interpretation:** *Do not use a test for something other than what it was designed for without taking care to ensure it is appropriate for the other purpose.*

The use of a single test for important decisions is equally reprehensible. No child should be placed in a gifted and talented program or retained in grade on the basis of a single test. The assignment of a student to special education services through a single test, of course, violates the law.

> **Principle of Data Interpretation:** *Do not make important decisions about individuals or groups on the basis of a single test.*

Given the current obsession with tests, we are likely to see the *Inevitable Corruption of Indicators and Educators Through High-Stakes Testing,* to use the title of a monograph by Sharon Nichols and David Berliner (2005). We have so many examples of this corruption outside of education that it is depressing to think about them all at once: CEOs and their "creative accounting," athletes on steroids or making a farce of getting an education, ethical violations by politicians, scientific data altered to make the research sponsor's drug look more effective, and so forth.

I believe it was economist Richard Rothstein who first described the Russian shoe factory that made only small shoes—the reward system was based on how many pairs of shoes factories produced. Small shoes could be turned out faster than larger models, and the factory could point to more shoes per quantity of leather, too. In too many instances, the need to look good trumps any desire to do the right thing.

The Nichols-Berliner catalog of test-induced corruption is extensive and useful and I summarize the categories briefly here. Most, but not all, of the specific incidents come from other sources.

1. Administrator and Teacher Cheating. In Houston, a Wesley Elementary School teacher testified before the Houston Board of Education that after she returned from maternity leave, when time came to administer the Texas state test, her children were stunned that she wouldn't provide them the answers. She was called into the principal's office and told she apparently didn't know how to "administer a test The Wesley Way" (Benton and Hacker 2005).

Nichols and Berliner briefly describe eighty-three separate published stories on cheating, the overwhelming majority being dated from 1999 through 2004 (the monograph was published in early 2005).

2. Student Cheating. The results of a survey on cheating by high schoolers by the Josephson Institute for Ethics led me to title one of my monthly Research columns for *Phi Delta Kappan* "A Nation of Cheats" (Bracey 2005a). A company called Caveon does a healthy and growing business these days: it specializes in detecting cheating. A well-organized national cheating scandal on its life-determining college entrance exam rocked South Korea recently. (Koreans consider only three universities in the nation to be high prestige and these three have a collective admission rate of 1.87 percent. That is, fewer than two out of one hundred applicants are accepted.) In China, companies provide, for a price, substitutes to take crucial examinations. Usually the substitute is a person who has passed the exam or who scores well on tests generally. The companies first seek substitutes that look like the real candidate and fall back on fake IDs if none can be found. It is a growth industry.

Nichols and Berliner list twenty-six recent articles on homegrown student cheating.

3. Excluding Students from the Test. In Birmingham, Alabama, teacher Steve Orel pointed out to the media that the district had "administratively withdrawn" 522 low-scoring students just before the administration of the state test ("administratively withdrawn" means the kids had no say in the process). Birmingham fired him. He founded a school, now in its sixth year, to help these push-outs obtain GEDs and other certification. Scores went up in Birmingham, though, and several schools under threat of a state takeover avoided this fate. The superintendent received a bonus.

Historically many districts have excluded disabled students from taking the test or excluded their results from reports. No Child Left Behind has apparently greatly increased the number of students seeking GEDs. In some places, "bubble children"—those perceived as close to passing the test—are receiving extra attention while gifted children are ignored as are those deemed "hopeless cases" (Booher-Jennings 2005; Bracey 2005c).

Nichols and Berliner provide forty-eight examples in this category.

> Principle of Data Interpretation: *In analyzing test results,*
> *make certain that no students were improperly excluded from*
> *the testing.*

4. Misrepresentation of Dropout Data. In Houston, Robert Kimball, assistant principal of Sharpstown High School, observed that the school had more than one thousand freshmen, fewer than three hundred graduates, *and no dropouts.* Kimball told this to a local television station, which, as a CBS affiliate, relayed the story on to *60 Minutes* so the story got national play (60 Minutes II 2004). The district, in deep denial about the situation, relegated Kimball to an office with no work assignment and then transferred him to an elementary school. Kimball sued for two hundred thousand dollars and settled with the district for ninety-two thousand. He now teaches full-time at the University of Houston.[3]

The converse of low dropout rates in Houston was high college attendance. Sharpstown is a high-poverty high school but reported that 98.4 percent of its seniors went on to college. One other Houston principal stated that most of these students "couldn't spell college, let alone attend" (Schemo 2003, A14).

On pages 52–59 we discussed rates versus numbers, including an example from Massachusetts where the graduation rate was misrepresented because dropouts, push-outs, and other leavers were omitted.

Nichols and Berliner present eight stories.

5. Teaching to the Test. We have already seen perhaps the ultimate horror story of this phenomenon, the events from Prince George's County, Maryland (pages 143–144). The outcome there was similar to what was reported by Linda McNeil and Angela Valenzuela (2001) in Texas. They argued that many students could not use their reading skills outside of the Texas test context. And back on page 141 we noted a slightly more subtle curricular corruption, the onset of the five-sentence "essay."

6. Narrowing the Curriculum. Closely related to teaching to the tests are stories about the distortion of the curriculum. Some note that children in some schools now spend four hours on reading and mathematics, leaving

---

3. I thought this a rather paltry sum, but Kimball told me that in addition to the psychological stress of continued litigation, the legal fees of pursuing a larger settlement would have consumed most of any additional award.

little time for other topics (somehow, no one seems to realize that reading history, science, or social studies is reading, too). Other stories have lamented the loss of social studies, physical education, and art because they are not tested. Even nap time in kindergarten is under attack.

The Virginia Beach, Virginia, school board held a special meeting to decide if it needed to mandate recess in elementary schools because reports claimed many schools had abandoned it in order to give more prep time to the state tests. Tacoma, Washington, schools did eliminate recess. This is unfortunate, given evidence that recess is important to cognitive, social, and physical development (Pellegrini and Bohn 2005, Bracey 2005b).

In its last act before closing, the Council for Basic Education reported that American schools had suffered "academic atrophy" in social studies, history, geography, civics, languages, and the arts (von Zastrow 2004).

And, closely related to how the curriculum is narrowed are stories about restrictions on how the curriculum is taught. Scripted curricula are the order of the day, no innovation or improvisation allowed. There is no such thing as the teachable moment in such a system.

Nichols and Berliner describe thirteen stories.

> **Principle of Data Interpretation:** *In evaluating a testing program, look for negative or positive outcomes that are not part of the program. For example, are subjects not tested being neglected? Are scores on other tests showing gains or losses?*

Nichols and Berliner then add four additional consequences that seem to me not so much the inevitable corruptions of a high-stakes system, but what we might term the collateral damage inflicted because of the system(s) we do have.

7. Conflicting Accountability Ratings. The adequate yearly progress accountability provisions of No Child Left Behind are arbitrary in the capricious sense. There are no considered judgments behind them. It is not surprising, then, that the results from NCLB conflict with those emanating from state accountability systems, which, although often wrongheaded, too, have some thought supporting them. Perhaps the most amusing of these conflicts comes from Florida, where in 2004 three-quarters of the schools that received an A or a B in Governor Jeb Bush's A+ state accountability system received a failing grade from brother George Bush's federal system. Widespread conflicts were reported in Missouri, Oregon, Colorado, and California. Typically, more schools fail under NCLB than under a state system because of the draconian arbitrariness of NCLB—California projects that 99 percent of its schools will be labeled as failures by the year 2014, when 100 percent of students are required to be proficient. In high-scoring Minnesota the projection is for a "mere" 80 percent failure rate—using a good-case scenario, but for the six Great Lake states taken together, the average failure rate under the best conditions is 95 percent (Wiley, Mathis, and Garcia 2005.)

8. Changing Meaning of Proficiency. Given that each state uniquely defines *proficient* and given the capriciousness of NCLB, it is not surprising that different states have wildly varying proportions of students attaining proficient status or that students judged proficient by a state accountability system are judged lacking under NCLB. Some districts have threatened to award diplomas to students who fail state tests, arguing that a diploma is the prerogative of the district, not the state.

Some states that have high standards and, consequently, high NCLB failure rates have considered lowering their standards as well as cut scores, something Thomas Toch and others predicted at the outset. In New York, a given cut score was applied to a new Regents Math A test and more than 70 percent of ninth graders failed. Articles savaged the test makers (Winerip 2003). Fortunately, New York, unlike many states, does not keep its tests secret. After the administration, the state makes them available online. There was general agreement that the test was too hard and later forms were made easier. In Texas, the reverse has happened as the state changed from a relatively easy test to a more difficult one.

The outcome of Texas' shift will be interesting to watch, as the discrepancy between the percent of students labeled proficient by the earlier test and the percent so labeled by NAEP was the highest in the nation. Texas said 87 percent of its fourth graders were proficient in mathematics; NAEP said 33 percent (Mathews 2005b) (but see discussion of NAEP achievement levels on pages 149–151).

9. The Morale of School Personnel. The previous eight outcomes paint a picture of confusion. As noted on page 118, teachers have never considered standardized testing a valid measure of what they were all about. Given that, one might expect any increase on testing to increase stress on teachers, even without a dollop of negativity. But, of course, the negativity is there. There has been a steady stream of it since *A Nation at Risk,* and of course, NCLB is written wholly in terms of negative, not positive, outcomes.

Stories abound of teachers taking early retirement although no study has formally documented this phenomenon. What has been documented in places like New York is teachers trying to avoid grades in which high-stakes tests take place. Teachers there shun the third grade, and since veteran New York teachers get pretty free rein to choose their assignments, there is no doubt a sizable proportion of less experienced teachers in the third grade.

10. Errors of Scoring and Reporting. There have always been errors made in the scoring and reporting of test results. Often these have come to light accidentally. In Minnesota a father who wanted to assist his daughter who had failed the state test convinced the state to let him see the test and her answer sheet simultaneously. He discovered his daughter had not failed the test. A number of items had been miskeyed and the computer had scored the girl as getting them wrong when she had not. In fact, 47,000 Minnesota high school students had received lower grades than they deserved, 8,000 had failed when they should have passed, and 525 seniors had been wrongfully denied diplomas. NCS, the scoring company, settled a suit on behalf of all the wronged students for $7 million (Bowman 2000).

No doubt errors have increased because the quantity of testing has increased enormously and at the same time states insist on shorter times between administration of the tests and delivery of the scored data and reports. The Government Accounting Office (2003) noted that to meet the requirements of NCLB, most states would need to add tests and that they would spend $1.9 billion over a six-year period even if they used the cheapest possible format, multiple choice. And that was just to meet the NCLB requirements, which technically affect only those schools receiving Title I funds, about half the schools in the nation. But most districts test all schools, not just Title I schools. Taking all state testing into account, Eduventures, an education industry research and marketing firm, put the figure at $5.4 billion over the same six-year period (Olson 2004, 18–19).[4]

The NCS escapade might be the most notorious, but other large companies such as Harcourt Assessment and CTB/McGraw-Hill have been hit

---

4. Eduventures actually used a shorter time span. Eduventures' numbers indicated linear increases over a four-year period. To make this period the same as that analyzed by the GAO, I extrapolated Eduventures' numbers, assuming the linear increases in spending would continue.

with suits and contract cancellations as well. An error by CTB/McGraw-Hill resulted in more than 8,600 New York City third graders being wrongly forced to attend summer school (Archibold 1999). (NCS is now NCS Pearson. At the time of the error the company lacked adequate quality control because its CEO was deliberately keeping it short staffed in order to show high profits and make the company an attractive takeover target. The Pearson publishing empire bought it for $2.5 billion. The CEO reportedly pocketed $50 million from the deal. In any case, he retired immediately after the purchase.)

The Future of Testing

The testing with which America is obsessed is stupid testing. It tells us nothing of how children learn or how they think about what they know. Psychometrician Robert Mislevy captured our approach to testing with this pithy remark: "It is only a slight exaggeration to describe the test theory that dominates educational measurement today as the application of twentieth-century statistics to nineteenth-century psychology" (Fredericksen, Mislevy, and Bejar 1993, 9).

Actually, Mislevy might have been more accurate if he had ascribed the dominant theory to eighteenth-century psychology. The tenets of testing today reflect the musings of the group of late seventeenth- and eighteenth-century philosophers known as the British Empiricists: John Locke, Bishop George Berkeley, David Hume, and a number of lesser-known others.

And, really, Mislevy was being generous in stating that a *theory* underlies testing. The Committee on the Foundations of Assessment observed that "current assessments are derived from early theories that characterize learning as a step-by-step accumulation of facts, procedures, definitions, and other discrete bits of knowledge and skills" (National Research Council 2001, 26). Precisely.

The committee offered an example of a question and two student responses:

QUESTION: What was the date of the battle of the Spanish Armada?
STUDENT 1: 1588. (correct)
QUESTION: Can you tell me about what this meant?
STUDENT 1: Not much. It was one of the dates I memorized for the test.

QUESTION: What was the date of the battle of the Spanish Armada?

STUDENT 2: It must have been around 1590.

QUESTION: Why do you say that?

STUDENT 2: Well, I know the English began to settle in Virginia just after 1600, not sure of the exact date. They would not have dared start overseas settlements if Spain still had control of the seas. It would take a little while to get expeditions organized, so England must have gained naval supremacy somewhere in the late 1500s.

Student 2's dates are a little off, but his reasoning is impeccable. The English had challenged Spain before their victory over the Armada and, indeed, Spain's Phillip II sent the armada out as an attempt to strike a definitive blow and end the war with England in Spain's favor. England had explored Roanoke Island in 1584 and established a colony there (the Lost Colony) in 1585. But student 2 is able to think his way to a reasonable answer and, much more important, he sees the significance and the consequences of the British victory, something apparently missing from student 1's awareness. Most tests today, though, would likely favor student 1.

The exchange with student 2 requires an interaction with another person and brings us back into the area of performance testing. Which, if we really want to examine how people think or the rationales they give for answers, is where we need to be. Whether or not such performance testing can be suitably automated with computers to make large-scale assessment possible, though, is questionable.

The development of tests that get at what people really know and how people really think about what they know is proceeding, but more slowly than necessary because resources are flowing into ever more tests of the kind disparaged by Mislevy and the Committee on the Foundations of Assessment. One can only hope for speedy developments to end the mess we are in now.

Summing Up

O ne of the people who reviewed the first draft of this book said that I had given her an "incredible collection of trees" and she was now wondering if I could draw them together as a forest. I lack a powerful theme to bring all this together, but it seems to me that the importance of being a savvy consumer of statistics goes well beyond educational research and the earlier analyzed world of advertising. Indeed, a number of illustrations in the book came from reporters and columnists writing outside the field of education. If I controlled the curriculum, I'd order up course or a multigrade thread in consumer-oriented probability and statistics, maybe even replacing one of the traditional math courses.

People are constantly reminding us that we suffer now from too much information from too many sources. And, thanks to the Internet, none of us needs to be solely a passive recipient of statistics. We can seek out information now in ways that were not possible before the Internet became what it is. It would seem to me important to evaluate what's arriving before our eyes and ears.

I do think that Joel Best is right when he says that people accept statistics uncritically. A few probably go to the other extreme and reject all statistics, taking the dismissive stance that you can prove anything with statistics. I hope the principles in this book and the exposition surrounding them will go some ways to making Best's statement wrong in the future.

I would be happy to hear from any reader suggestions for what a second edition of this book might add, delete, alter, or reorganize. Maybe there's a forest in here somewhere.

Resources

Interpreting Statistics

Best, Joel. 2001. *Damned Lies and Statistics.* Berkeley: University of California Press.

———. 2004. *More Damned Lies and Statistics.* Berkeley: University of California Press.

Huff, Darrell. 1954. *How to Lie with Statistics.* New York: W. W. Norton.

Data Mining

Holcomb, Edie. 2004. *Getting Excited About Data.* 2d ed. Thousand Oaks, CA: Corwin.

Streifer, Philip. 2004. *Tools and Techniques for Effective Data-Driven Decision Making.* Lanham, MD: Scarecrow.

Understanding Graphs

Tufte, Edward R. 2001. *The Visual Display of Quantitative Information.* 2d ed. Cheshire, CT: Graphics.

Wainer, Howard. 2000. *Visual Revelations: Graphical Tales of Fate and Deception from Napoleon Bonaparte to Ross Perot.* 2d ed. Hillsdale, NJ: Erlbaum.

———. 2005. *Graphic Discovery.* Princeton, NJ: Princeton University Press.

The Ins and Outs of Testing

Heubert, James P., and Robert Hauser. 1999. *High Stakes: Testing for Tracking, Promotion and Graduation.* Washington, DC: National Academy Press.

Kohn, Alfie. 2000. *The Case Against Standardized Testing.* Portsmouth, NH: Heinemann.

Popham, W. James. 2000. *Modern Educational Measurement: Practical Guidelines for Educational Leaders.* Boston: Allyn & Bacon.

Wiggins, Grant P. 1993. *Assessing Student Performance.* San Francisco: Jossey-Bass.

Works Cited

Alexander, Lamar, and H. Thomas James. 1987. *The Nation's Report Card: Improving the Assessment of Student Achievement.* Cambridge, MA: National Academy of Education.

Angoff, William F., ed. 1970. *The College Board Admissions Testing Program: A Technical Report on Research and Development Activities in Relation to the Scholastic Aptitude Test and Achievement Tests.* New York: College Entrance Examination Board.

Archibold, Randal C. 1999. "Board Now Says Summer School Was Wrongly Ordered for 8,600." *New York Times,* 16 September, A1.

Arendt, Hannah. 1963. *Eichmann in Jerusalem: A Report on the Banality of Evil.* New York: Viking.

Belfield, Clive, and Chad d'Entremont. 2005. "Will Disadvantaged Students Benefit from a Free Market in Educational Services?" *American School Board Journal* (April): 28–31.

Bell, Terrel. 1988. *The Thirteenth Man: A Reagan Cabinet Memoir.* New York: Free Press.

Bennett, William J. 2000. "Critical Courses." *Washington Post,* 4 September, A25.

Benton, Joshua, and Holly K. Hacker. 2005. "Celebrated School Accused of Cheating." *Dallas Morning News,* 31 March. Retrieved at www.dallasnews.com/sharedcontent/dws/news/longterm/stories /123104dnmetcheating.add1e.html.

Best, Joel. 2001. *Damned Lies and Statistics.* Berkeley: University of California Press.

———. 2004. *More Damned Lies and Statistics.* Berkeley: University of California Press.

Bingham, Judith. 2005. "Texas Teacher Is Fed Up with Retention and TAKS." www.educationnews.org/texas-teacher-is-feedup-with.htm.

Bloom, Benjamin H. 1971. "Mastery Learning." In *Mastery Learning: Theory and Practice,* ed. James H. Block. New York: Holt, Rinehart and Winston.

Bloom, Benjamin, George Madaus, and Thomas Hastings. 1981. *Evaluation to Improve Learning.* New York: McGraw-Hill.

Booher-Jennings, Jennifer. 2005. "Below the Bubble: 'Educational Triage' and the Texas Accountability System." *American Educational Research Journal* (Summer): 231–68.

Bowman, Darcia Harris. 2000. "Minn. Extends Testing Contract Despite Scoring Mistakes." Retrieved at www.edweek.org/ew/articles/2000/09/06/01minn.h20.html (August 13, 2005).

Bracey, Gerald W. 1993. "George Will's Urban Legend." *Education Week* (September 29): 29.

———. 2005a. "A Nation of Cheats." *Phi Delta Kappan* (January): 412–13.

———. 2005b. "The Power of Monkey Bars." *Phi Delta Kappan* (November): 253–54.

———. 2005c. "Blowing Bubbles in Texas." *Phi Delta Kappan* (December): 333–35.

Brigham, Carl Campbell. 1926. "The Scholastic Aptitude Test of the College Entrance Examination Board." In *The Work of the College Entrance Examination Board, 1901–1925,* ed. T. S. Fiske. New York: Ginn.

Broder, David. 2005. "The Metrics of Success in Iraq." *Washington Post,* 3 July, B7.

Brooke, James. 2005. "China's Economic Brawn Unsettles Japanese." *New York Times,* 27 June, C1.

Campbell, David T. 1975. "Assessing the Impact of Planned Social Change." In *Social Research and Public Policies: The Dartmouth/OECD Conference,* ed. G. Lyons, 3–45. Hanover, NH: Public Affairs Center, Dartmouth College.

Carnevale, Anthony P., and Donna M. Desrochers. 2004. *Standards for What? The Economic Roots of K–16 Reform.* Princeton, NJ: Educational Testing Service.

Carson, Charles, Robert Huelskamp, and Thomas Woodall. 1993. "Perspectives on Education in America." *Journal of Educational Research* (May/June): 259–310.

Center for Consumer Freedom. 2005. "Declaration of Food Independence." Retrieved from www.consumerfreedom.com/article_detail.cfm?article=155 (July 4, 2005).

Cohen, Michael, and Matthew Gandal. 2004. *Do Graduation Tests Measure Up?* Washington, DC: Achieve, Inc.

Coleman, James S. 1966. *Equality of Education Opportunity Study.* Washington, DC: Department of Health, Education, and Welfare.

Cronbach, Lee J. 1960. *Essentials of Psychological Testing.* 2d ed. New York: Harper & Row.

Doyle, Denis P. 1995. *Where Connoisseurs Send Their Children to School: An Analysis of 1990 Census Data to Determine Where School Teachers Send Their Children to School.* Washington, DC: Center for Education Reform.

Doyle, Denis P., Brian Diepold, and David Alan Deschryver. 2004. *Where Do Public School Teachers Send Their Children to School?* Washington, DC: Thomas B. Fordham Foundation.

Education Week. 1993. "Charting a Course to Reform: The Next Ten Years." Editorial (February 10).

Fernandez, Icess. 2005. "Every Pupil Counts in Testing to Meet Federal Standards." *Corpus Christi Caller Times,* 15 May, 1.

Florida Times–Union. 1998. "Allowing Choice." *Florida Times–Union,* 7 July, A10.

Frahm, Robert. 1979. *What's Happening in Minimum Competency Testing?* Washington, DC: George Washington Institute for Educational Leadership, George Washington University.

Fredericksen, Norman, Robert Mislevy, and Isaac A. Bejar, eds. 1993. *Test Theory for a New Generation of Tests.* Hillsdale, NJ: Lawrence Erlbaum.

Gardner, Howard. 1983. *Frames of Mind.* New York: Basic Books.

Gitomer, Drew, Andrew S. Latham, and Robert Ziomek. 1999. *The Academic Quality of Prospective Teachers: The Impact of Admissions and Licensure Testing.* Princeton, NJ: Educational Testing Service.

Gould, Stephen J. 1981. *The Mismeasure of Man.* New York: W. W. Norton.

Government Accounting Office (GAO). 2003. *Characteristics of Tests Will Influence Expenses.* GAO-03–089. Washington, DC: Government Accounting Office.

Greene, Jay P., Greg Forster, and Marcus A. Winters. 2003. *Apples to Apples: An Evaluation of Charter Schools Serving General Student Populations.* New York: Center for Civic Education, Manhattan Institute, July, Working Paper No. 1.

Harwood, Richard. 1994. "Reporting by, on, and for an Elite." *Washington Post,* 14 August, A29.

Hegarty, Stephen. 2003. "He Proffers the Proof in Voucher Fights." *St Petersburg Times,* 8 September, 1.

Holcomb, Edie. 2004. *Getting Excited About Data,* 2d ed. Thousand Oaks, CA: Corwin Press.

Hopkins, Jim. 2004. "Wal-Mart Heirs Pour Riches into Education Reform." *USA Today,* 11 March.

Horton, Paula. 2005. "Superintendent Calls Boy's Suspension a Mistake." *The Daily World,* 13 May, A1.

Hoffman, Banesh. 1964. *The Tyranny of Testing.* New York: Collier.

Huff, Darrell. 1954. *How to Lie with Statistics.* New York: W. W. Norton.

Johnson, William B., and Arnold E. Packer. 1987. *Workforce 2000: Work and Workers for the Twenty-first Century.* Indianapolis, IN: Hudson Institute.

Kahn, Chris. 2005. "Despite Law, Some Pupils Left Behind." *South Florida Sun Sentinel,* 8 July, B1.

Kennedy, Robert F. Jr. 2004. Speech given at Fighting Bob Fest, Baraboo, Wisconsin, 18 September.

Klugh, Henry E. 1986. *Statistics: The Essentials of Research.* 3d ed. Hillsdale, NJ: Lawrence Erlbaum.

Krugman, Paul. 2005a. "Design for Confusion." *New York Times,* 5 August, A15.

———. 2005b. "Girth of a Nation." *New York Times,* 4 July, A17.

Le, Cecilia. 2005. "Test Scoring to Change for Delaware Schools." *News Journal,* 21 October.

Lemann, Nicholas. 1999. *The Big Test: The Secret History of the SAT.* New York: Farrar, Straus & Giroux.

Mathews, Jay. 2005a. "D.C. Family Finds Voucher Journey Well Worth It." *Washington Post,* 31 May, A1.

———. 2005b. "A Report Card with Rare Meaning." *Washington Post,* 7 June. Retrieved at www.washingtonpost.com/wp-dyn/content/article/2005/06/07/AR2005060700539.html

McNeil, Linda, and Angela Valenzuela. 2001. "The Harmful Impact of the TAAS System of Testing in Texas." In *Raising Standards or Raising Barriers? Inequality and High-Stakes Testing in Public Education,* ed. Gary Orfield and Mindy Kornhaber. New York: Century Foundation.

Mencken, H. L. No date. Quotes retrieved from www.brainyquotes.com/quotes /authors/h/h_l_mencken.html (July 2, 2005).

Millman, Jason. 1994. "Criterion-Referenced Testing 20 Years Late: Promises Broken, Promises Kept." *Educational Measurement: Issues and Practices* (Winter): 19.

Moe, Michael. 2005. E-mail correspondence with author.

Murray, Charles, and Richard Herrnstein. 1992. "What's Really Behind the SAT-Score Decline?" *Public Interest* (Winter): 32–56.

National Commission on Excellence in Education. 1983. *A Nation at Risk.* Washington, DC: U.S. Department of Education.

National Research Council. 2001. *Knowing What Students Know: The Science and Design of Educational Assessment.* Washington, DC: National Academy Press.

Nichols, Sharon L., and David C. Berliner. 2005. *The Inevitable Corruption of Indicators and Educators Through High-Stakes Testing.* Tempe, AZ: Arizona State University, Education Policy Research Unit. Retrieved at www.asu.edu/educ /epsl/EPRU/documents/EPSL-0503–101-EPRU.pdf

Olson, Lynn. 2004. "Law Bestows Bounty on Test Industry." *Education Week* (December 1): 18–19.

Orwell, George. 1950. "Politics and the English Language" (1946). In *Shooting an Elephant and Other Essays,* 77–92. New York: Harcourt Brace.

Pellegrini, Anthony N., and Catherine M. Bohn. 2005. "The Role of Recess in Children's Cognitive Performance and School Adjustment." *Educational Researcher* (January/February): 13–19.

Popham, W. James. 2000. *Modern Educational Measurement.* Boston: Allyn & Bacon.

Powell, Brian, and Lala Carr Steelman. 1996. "Bewitched, Bothered and Bewildering: The Use and Misuse of State SAT Scores." *Harvard Educational Review* (Fall): 26–59.

Raspberry, William. 2005. "No Clarity About Iraq." *Washington Post,* 4 July, A17.

Romainville, Marc. 2002. "On the Appropriate Use of PISA." *Nouvelle Revue* (Brussels) (March–April): 86–99.

Rothstein, Richard. 2004. "Testing Our Patience." In *Schools and Class,* 91. Washington, DC: Economic Policy Institute.

Rouse, Karen. 2005. "Students Who Balk at CSAP Held Back." *Denver Post,* 30 March, A1.

Sacchetti, Maria. 2005. "Colleges Question MCAS Success: Many in State Schools Still Need Remedial Help." *Boston Globe,* 26 June, A1.

Schemo, Diana Jean. 2003. "For Houston Schools, College Claims Exceed Reality." *New York Times,* 28 August, A14.

Shermer, Michael. 2005. "Turn Me On, Dead Man." *Scientific American* (May): 37.

60 Minutes II. 2004. "The Texas Miracle." Retrieved at www.cbsnews.com /stories/2004/01/06/60II/main591676.shtml (July 27, 2005).

Streifer, Philip. 2004. *Tools and Techniques for Effective Data-Driven Decision Making.* Lanham, MD: Scarecrow Education.

Toch, Thomas. 2001. "Bush's Big Test." *Washington Monthly* (November): 12–17.

UNICEF. 2005. *Child Poverty in Rich Countries 2005.* Florence, Italy: Innocenti Research Centre, UNICEF.

U.S. Department of Education. 1996. *Out of the Lecture Hall and into the Classroom: 1992–93 College Graduates and Elementary/Secondary Teaching.* Washington, DC: National Center for Education Statistics, August, Report No. NCES 96–899.

Viadero, Debra. 2005. "Release of Unreviewed Studies Sparks Debate." *Education Week* (May 18): 1.

von Zastrow, Claus. 2004. *Academic Atrophy: The Condition of Liberal Arts in America's Schools.* Report out of print. Summary of findings appeared as a commentary in *Education Week* by Raymond Bartlett and Claus von Zastrow. Retrieved at www.edweek.org/ew/articles/2004/0407/30bartlett.h23.html ?querystring-zastow (July 27, 2005).

Wainer, Howard. 2000. *Visual Revelations: Graphic Tales of Fate and Deception from Napoleon Bonaparte to Ross Perot.* Mahwah, NJ: Lawrence Erlbaum Associates.

Wainer, Howard, and Daniel Koretz. 2003. "Visual Revelations." *Chance* (Fall).

Wheelock, Anne. 2004. "Massachusetts Department of Education 'Progress Report' Inflates 'Pass Rates' for Class of 2004." www.massparents.org/news /2004/passrate_2004.htm

Wiley, Edward W., William J. Mathis, and David R. Garcia. 2005. *The Impact of the Adequate Yearly Progress Requirement of the Federal "No Child Left Behind" Act on Schools in the Great Lakes Region.* Tempe, AZ: Education Policy Studies Laboratory, Arizona State University. Retrieved from www.asu.edu/educ /epsl/EPRU/documents/EPSL-0509–109-EPRU.pdf

Will, George F. 1993a. "Meaningless Money Factor." *Washington Post,* 24 September, A22.

———. 1993b. "Taking Back Education." *Washington Post,* 26 August, A27.

———. 1993c. "When the State Fails Its Citizens." *Washington Post,* 7 March, C7.

———. 2001. "Holden Caulfield, American Whiner." *Washington Post,* 1 July, B7.

———. 2005. "Is Embarrassment the Right Lever?" *Washington Post,* 23 June, A27.

Winerip, Michael. 2003. "A 70 Percent Failure Rate? Try Testing the Testers." *New York Times,* 25 June, B9.

———. 2005a. "SAT Essay Test Rewards Length and Ignores Errors." *New York Times,* 4 May, B9.

———. 2005b. "Test Scores Are Up, So Why Isn't Everybody Happy?" *New York Times,* 29 June, B9.

World Economic Forum. 2005. *Global Competitiveness Report, 2004–2005.* Geneva, Switzerland: World Economic Forum.

Wood, John. 2005. "Here Are the Reasons I Didn't Graduate from Federal Hocking Last Weekend." *Athens* (Ohio) *News,* 2 June. www.athensnews.com /issue/article/php3?story_id=20780

Index